MUSIC LAB

WE ROCK!

A Fun Family Guide for Exploring Rock Music History

Jason Hanley

Quarry Books
100 Cummings Center, Suite 406L
Beverly, MA 01915
quarrybooks.com • craftside.typepad.com

First published in the United States of America in 2015 by
Quarry Books, a member of
Quarto Publishing Group USA Inc.
100 Cummings Center
Suite 406-L
Beverly, Massachusetts 01915-6101
Telephone: (978) 282-9590
Fax: (978) 283-2742
www.quarrybooks.com

10 9 8 7 6 5 4 3 2 1

ISBN: 978-1-59253-921-5

Digital edition published in 2015
eISBN: 978-1-62788-220-0

Library of Congress Cataloging-in-Publication Data

Hanley, Jason (Musician)
Music lab: We rock! : a fun family guide for exploring rock music history /
    Jason Hanley.
    pages cm
    Includes index.
  ISBN 978-1-59253-921-5
1. Rock music--Analysis, appreciation. 2. Rock music--History and criticism.
    I. Title.
  MT146.H38 2015
  781.6609--dc23
  2014024876

Design: Leigh Ring // www.ringartdesign.com
Cover images: Front cover: Tuan Tran/gettyimages.com, (top, left); Redferns/gettyimages.com, (top, right);
Kidstock/gettyimages.com, (bottom, left & right). Back jacket: Janet Makosca, (top, left & bottom);
Michael Ochs Archives/gettyimages.com, (top, right)

Printed in China

FOR MY
⤙ ROCK AND ROLL ⤚
FAMILY

CHRISTINE, MAISIE, ELLA, HANNAH, AND BURKE

CONTENTS

-⚡ INTRODUCTION ⚡-
WHAT'S THIS BOOK ALL ABOUT?

You may be asking yourself, "Why do I need a book about the history of rock and roll when everything I could want is available on the Internet?" Well, I would suggest that is *the* reason you need a book like this. Now that we have unprecedented access to music in a way no one has ever had before, it affects our habits as listeners. We can listen to an amazing previously unavailable back catalog of music. We can hear music that used to be played in only one part of the world. We might even hear new sounds we have never heard before. But on the other hand, we might be confronted by too many choices. For example, if I simply type "James Brown" into Google, it brings up 366 million results, and even if I take time to sort through all of that, I might end up with thousands of opinions about what to listen to or think about James Brown. If I just type in "Funk" (the style of music most closely associated with James Brown), it results in another 250 million websites. You get the idea. The point is this: I've done the work for you already. This book gives you the places to start, a road map to move further along, and a listening guide to help you learn how to hear everything rock and roll has to offer.

In our growing digital world, social media can bring people together, but it also has an equal power to pull us apart. That's why this book is called a *family* listening guide. Don't read this book alone and keep it to yourself. Don't listen to the music in the dark with earbud headphones on your iPod/iPad/iPhone (or whatever digital music device you have). Share this music with your spouse, your kids, your friends—and don't share it by only posting about it on Facebook (although you can do that too if you want). Play the music in the living room, in the car, at the beach, in the backyard, and listen to it—together (and if at all possible at high volume). This book is a journey. It gives you fifty-two starting points, fifty-two places you can begin a musical odyssey, and if you like them all, you can keep going down each of those paths. Maybe you will only like forty-five of them. That's fine.

I didn't write this book to name the "best" songs ever for everyone. In some cases, I didn't even pick the most popular song by a particular musician. Instead, I picked the song I think people might respond the most to, the song that gets them to share and interact with one another, the song to get them up and shaking their stuff. Because let's face it, if we all made a list of the "best" songs we ever heard, each list would be a little different—because we are all different. So come on the journey with me. Listen to the tunes (more on that shortly). Think about the stories of the musicians who made it, where they came from, and how they changed the world. Try out the activities and see what happens when you and your family spend some time together with music. Maybe it'll be like my house where inevitably one of my kids shouts out, "this is *my* song"—which means it's their turn to sing the lead. And don't forget that sometimes it is *your* turn to sing lead, too. Long live the Rock!

⭐ Find the **We Rock! Book** playlists on Spotify and Songza to listen to all the songs featured in this book.

Opposite Page: Pink Floyd live, 1990 (top); Michael Jackson, (bottom, left); Depeche Mode, Berlin, 1984, (bottom, right)

HOW TO
⌐ LISTEN CAREFULLY ⌐

If you're reading this book, then chances are you already enjoy listening to music. But I want you to try and listen *carefully*. It's about focusing on the sounds and hearing the details. You may have done it before. Have you ever gone back and listened to a song you've played a hundred times and suddenly you notice a new instrument you've never heard before? That's what I want you to try and do. To help you with that, each Lab in this book features a Listening Guide for one song. In most cases, it is the "single" version of the song, but in some cases where I have picked something else, I have noted it. Listen to the song together as a family and follow along with the Listening Guide. It has time references listed as minutes:seconds to help you find your place. Each one will ask you to listen for the musical form, instrumentation, rhythm, pitch, and timbre in the music. You can't do all of that by listening to the song just once, so make sure to do some repeated listening so you have the opportunity to focus on various aspects of the music. And don't forget that you're also listening because it's fun!

HOW TO
⌐ HAVE FUN AS A FAMILY ⌐ WITH MUSIC

This book is filled with fun ideas about how to enjoy music as a family. Listen together as a group, and share your thoughts—what you hear, what you feel, what you think about the song. Play along and don't worry if you're good or not. Nobody ever got good at anything by *not* doing it. And trust me, the kids will love it. Some of the "Try This At Home" activities ask you to do things that relate to the social and historical context of the music. Feel free to expand or experiment on your own to come up with other cool new ideas (and let me know what you come up with). The "Rock Destinations" sections will give you ideas for fun musical trips you can take. Make music a joyous experience in your family and then share it with your friends.

CHAPTER 1:
⚡ ROCK & ROLL ⚡
BASICS

Ron Wood and Keith Richards, The Rolling Stones, 1978

ELVIS PRESLEY

Played: **ROCK AND ROLL**

PLAYLIST

"That's All Right" (1954)

"Mystery Train" (1955)

"Hound Dog" (1956)

"Heartbreak Hotel" (1956)

"Love Me Tender" (1956)

"All Shook Up" (1957)

"(Let Me Be Your) Teddy Bear" (1957)

"Jailhouse Rock" (1957)

"It's Now or Never" (1960)

"Return to Sender" (1962)

"Viva Las Vegas" (1964)

"Suspicious Minds" (1969)

"Burning Love" (1972)

DESTINATIONS

If you're planning on taking a trip and want to go to the one place that is the center of the Elvis universe, then head on out to Memphis, Tennessee, to visit the actual home of Elvis Presley, Graceland.

Elvis Aaron Presley (1935–1977) was not the very first musician to play rock and roll, but he was the first to reach a level of mega-stardom—something that helped to popularize the music around the world. He was born in Tupelo, Mississippi, and moved to Memphis, Tennessee, when he was thirteen. In 1953, he walked into the Memphis Recording Service, owned by Sam Phillips, to record two songs (allegedly as a gift for his mother), and by July of 1954 he recorded his first single for Phillip's Sun Records, "That's All Right" backed with "Blue Moon of Kentucky." By 1956, he was making appearances on national television, recording for RCA records, and staring in movies such as *Love Me Tender* (1956). He soon gained his nickname as the "King of Rock and Roll."

HISTORICAL FACT/SOCIAL CONNECTIONS

While you're listening to the music of Elvis, stop and think about the world around him during the mid-1950s. Rock and roll music was still brand new, and it combined the sounds of other styles of American music that had been around for some time—like rhythm and blues, country, gospel, blues, and popular song. Elvis loved all these kinds of music and often mixed them together—something that did not always sit well with the racially divided United States at the time. His rockin' sound and dance moves drove teens wild and made many adults angry.

Released on RCA Records as a single, July 1956

Written by Jerry Leiber and Mike Stoller

This song is a true classic of Rock and roll music. It represents what was new and exciting in the 1950s—the combination of multiple musical traditions. The song was written in 1952 by Jerry Leiber and Mike Stoller who were one of rock and roll's earliest songwriting teams. They would later go on to write such classics as "Yakety Yak" for the Coasters and "On Broadway" for the Drifters (among others). "Hound Dog" was first recorded by rhythm and blues singer Willie Mae "Big Mama" Thornton in 1953 on Peacock Records. She was a powerful singer and songwriter (who also wrote and recorded the song "Ball n' Chain" which was made famous in rock circles by Janis Joplin). Elvis first heard the song performed by the group Freddie Bell and the Bellboys at the Sands Hotel and Casino while he was visiting Las Vegas in 1956 and then decided to perform it on *The Milton Berle Show* on June 5, 1956. That performance was both a major success, bringing national attention to Elvis and his music, and the cause of a major controversy, because many viewers found his dancing to be lewd and outrageous. Elvis and his band recorded the song the next day and it became a smash hit record. It was released only as a 45 rpm single and never appeared on an original Elvis LP.

Elvis performing on The Milton Berle Show. Written by Jerry Leiber and Mike Stoller. Released on RCA Records as a single, July 1956

TRY THIS AT HOME

Start by listening together as a group. Try to clap along to the beat: 1, 2, 3, 4—1, 2, 3, 4. Can you all stay in sync with each other and the song? Can you sing the melody of the song?

LISTENING GUIDE

"HOUNDDOG"

This song has a basic musical form that is called a 12 bar blues. These twelve measures of music repeat to make up the entire song, and each of these repetitions is called a verse. "Hound Dog" is a total of eight verses long, but because not all of them are exactly the same, we can practice listening by using the chart below. For those of you who can play music, this is a very easy song to play along with on guitar or keyboard. It is in the key of C major and uses the following chords (one for each measure): C, C, C, C, F, F, C, C, G, F, C, C.

0:00 | Verse 1 | Listen for the instruments playing in this section performed by Elvis's famous backing band: Guitar (Scotty Moore), Upright Bass (Bill Black), and Drums (D. J. Fontana). The backing singers also add a fun handclap rhythm to the song (see if you can clap along with it). Elvis sings the song's lyrics that tell the story of a dog that is not doing what it is supposed to be doing. Think about the words. Do you think that Elvis is really singing about a dog? What is another way that we can interpret these lyrics? Listen to the way that Elvis sings the song. He sounds excited. And his voice is a little rough or scratchy—this is what is called the timbre of the voice.

0:17 | Verse 2 | This verse features the same music but with a new set of lyrics.

0:34 | Verse 3 | Again, same music but Elvis returns to the lyrics from verse 1.

0:50 | Guitar Solo 1 with backing vocals from the Jordanaires Notice that the guitar, bass, and drums still play almost the same thing as the first three verses, but with no break at the end.

1:06 | Verse 4

1:23 | Guitar Solo 2 with backing vocals from the Jordanaires

1:40 | Verse 5

1:56 | Verse 6

Ends with a quick stop.

CHUCK BERRY

Played: **ROCK AND ROLL**

Chuck Berry (born 1926 in St. Louis, Missouri) was one of the great stars of early rock and roll. His big break came in 1955 when blues musician Muddy Waters introduced him to Leonard Chess of Chess Records. Berry was a triple threat: a gifted guitar player, an energetic performer, and a skilled songwriter. His guitar playing was rooted in rhythm and blues, but he put a twist on it that gave birth to rock and roll guitar—take a listen to the opening of "Johnny B. Goode" if you need proof. His signature performance move, "the duck walk," drove audiences wild as he scooted across the stage with his guitar in hand cranking out guitar solos. As a songwriter, he was able to capture in his music and lyrics the essence of 1950s American teenage life—despite the fact that Berry himself was already in his twenties. Even students in the twenty-first century can listen to the music of "School Days" and relate to the story (just replace the desire to listen to music on the jukebox with mobile devices).

- PLAYLIST -

"Maybellene" (1955)

"You Can't Catch Me" (1956)

"Roll Over Beethoven" (1956)

"School Days" (1957)

"Rock and Roll Music" (1957)

"Sweet Little Sixteen" (1958)

"Johnny B. Goode" (1958)

"Memphis, Tennessee" (1959)

"Nadine" (1964)

"No Particular Place to Go" (1964)

"Tulane" (1970)

HISTORICAL FACT/SOCIAL CONNECTIONS

Rock and roll artists like Elvis Presley pushed at the acceptable boundaries of 1950s American culture by mixing R&B, gospel, and country, and by performing in a suggestive manner. But an artist like Chuck Berry faced cultural obstacles of an entirely different kind. As an African American performer, he often met with prejudice when on tour. In his autobiography, Berry, describes a time when he had been scheduled to perform at a club in the South that had assumed he was white based on what they perceived to be the "country" sound of his music. When he showed up to play the gig, he was told he could not even enter the establishment because of a city ordinance that restricted black performers. Berry was forced to sit outside while the white backing band hired to play with him performed his songs to a sold out audience.

SONG FACTS: "ROCK AND ROLL MUSIC" (1957)

Written by Chuck Berry

Released on Chess Records, September 1957

Berry was such a great songwriter because he wrote songs about things that teens could relate to, including a rock and roll song that is about loving rock and roll. In his autobiography, Berry said, "I wanted the lyrics to define every aspect of [rock and roll's] being. . . ." In the lyrics, he mentions some of the most important musical ideas of rock and roll, such as one of the key

rhythmic aspects called the backbeat. He comments on how strong that particular rhythm is: "You can't lose it." The instruments we hear are very common in rock and roll: guitar, piano, drums, and bass.

Chuck Berry performs the "duck walk" on the TAMI show, December 29, 1964

Because Berry's guitar and voice are so dominant in his songs, many people don't listen to the amazing piano work of Johnny Johnson, so make sure to pay attention to it in this song.

TRY THIS AT HOME

Try writing some rock and roll lyrics of your own. Berry wrote lyrics about the things he observed around him, things that teens cared about. Think about what is important to you and your family and try to come up with some ideas. Don't worry about writing it in verse just yet. Are you stuck? Don't worry. There are rock and roll songs about everything from relationships to taking out the trash. If you need help getting started, then try something simple like updating Berry's song "School Days" to reflect modern times and the things that your children face in school every day.

Once you have good ideas on paper, then think about how you can group them into a story. Listen to "Rock and Roll Music" again, and notice how in each verse Chuck Berry talks about a different musical idea (modern jazz, saxophone, Latin dance music), and how the chorus always comes back to the same idea—that rock and roll is his favorite. Now try to group your story in the same way. Write out some lyrics, short phrases that have a rhyme pattern, like, "Every day we have to do chores. Cleaning my room is such a bore. All I want to do is have fun and play. Let's rock and roll night and day."

LISTENING GUIDE

This song has a basic musical form that alternates back and forth between a sung verse and a repeated chorus.

0:00 | Chorus 1 | After a short strummed guitar introduction, the song begins with the chorus—a smart idea to put the repeated hook right up front. The drums, piano, guitar, and bass play, and all of them have some amount of echo on the sound.

0:22 | Verse 1 | In the verses, Berry sings about several different types of music. In this verse, he says he likes modern jazz, but sometimes when the band plays it too fast it loses the beauty of the melody—what a great musical observation. The music changes in the verses to strummed guitar chords. This helps to differentiate it from the rock and roll of the chorus.

0:35 | Chorus 2 | Same as chorus 1. Listen to the high notes in the piano that play an entirely different melody from the one that Berry is singing.

0:54 | Verse 2 | In this verse, Berry talks about taking his girlfriend to hear a rocking band with an amazing saxophone player. Check out the great forced rhyme that makes "band" rhyme with "hurricane."

1:06 | Chorus 3 |

1:25 | Verse 3 | The setting is a country jamboree down south (maybe a reference to his love of country music), but once the party starts to get going, they play rock and roll.

1:38 | Chorus 4 |

1:56 | Verse 4 | In the last verse, Berry mentions how he doesn't care to listen to the many Latin-inspired dance craze songs of the '50s—the tango, the mambo. Notice that the music played by the band changes at this point to mimic a Latin dance rhythm (a great way to connect the music and the lyrics).

2:09 | Chorus 5 | Don't miss the fact that as soon as Berry calls out the piano at the end of verse 4, "Keep rockin' that piano," Johnson pulls out all the stops during his performance in the last chorus. This chorus is the same as the others but adds a brief extension to the ending as a way to finish the song.

⌐ PLAYLIST ⌐

"The Fat Man" (1949)

"Mardi Gras in New Orleans" (1953)

"Ain't That a Shame" (1955)

"I'm in Love Again" (1956)

"Blueberry Hill" (1956)

"Blue Monday" (1956)

"I'm Walking" (1957)

"I Want to Walk You Home" (1959)

"Walking to New Orleans" (1960)

"Jambalaya" (1961)

Fats Domino (b. 1928) is one of New Orleans's favorite sons and one of the all-time great rock and roll piano players. He has lived his entire life in New Orleans, and despite his fame, most of that time has been spent in the Lower Ninth Ward (a working-class neighborhood). His sweet voice, rolling piano playing, and delightful charisma on stage made him a star around the world. Domino was second only to Elvis in the number of hit records sold during the 1950s. The majority of Domino's songs were recorded at J&M Studios and made with producer and trumpet player Dave Bartholomew, who also served as Domino's bandleader. Members of the band included top-level musicians such as Herb Hardesty (sax), Billy Diamond (bass), Lee Allen (sax), Cornelius Coleman (drums), Walter Nelson (guitar), and Ernest McLean (guitar). All of them helped to shape the sound of rock and roll in the early 1950s—in fact, it is often said that "The Fat Man" from 1949 may be the first song to ever be recorded with rock and roll's famous backbeat.

Dave Bartholomew plays trumpet outside of the J&M Studios building.

HISTORICAL FACT/SOCIAL CONNECTIONS

While you're listening to the music of Fats Domino, think about the nature of his home city. New Orleans is a port city on the banks of the Mississippi River, and as such it played a major role in the Atlantic slave trade in the United States. J&M Studios where Fats Domino recorded much of his music was across the street from the historic Congo Square (a location where slaves were allowed to free associate on Sundays starting in the eighteenth century). Latin beats, African rhythms, jazz music, rhythm and blues—all of these crossed paths in the jambalaya of the city. Nightclubs like the Dew Drop Inn allowed musicians to perform for local crowds and perfect their sound.

SONG FACTS: "BLUE MONDAY" (1956)

Written by Dave Bartholomew and Fats Domino

Released on Imperial Records, 1956

This song demonstrates the sound of early rhythm and blues–inspired rock and roll with piano, drums, saxophone, bass, and voice. Listen to how clear Domino's voice is as he sings the main melody. His evocative narrative pulls us into the song. The lyrics are a time-honored trope of working-class rock and roll. The singer works hard all week, and then on Saturday it's time to have fun. On Sunday, he feels tired from all the fun and needs to rest, but the bad part is that he has to go back to work on Monday—oh, that blue Monday. This Fats Domino song is one that almost anyone can relate to—and did I mention that it's only 2 minutes and 20 seconds long?

DESTINATIONS

The food and music of New Orleans is something to experience for yourself. Try eating some gumbo, jambalaya, and beignets while listening to the sounds of brass bands in the street, the Preservation Hall Jazz Band, and some killer rhythm and blues. Spend some time in the French Quarter and make sure to head toward the corner of N. Rampart and Dumaine, where you can see the original location of Cosimo Matassa's J&M recording studio and where so much of the city's best music was recorded. If you look closely, you'll see that the building has two historic landmarks: one from the city of New Orleans and another from the Rock and Roll Hall of Fame. Look down on the ground at the front door and you can still see the original brick work that says J&M. Inside the building, there are some photos in the back where the studio used to be.

LISTENING GUIDE

"BLUE MONDAY"

Domino plays the piano throughout using a triplet rhythm against the 4/4 timing of the rest of the band. The drums play a constant beat with the snare drum playing on the backbeat for most of the song. The saxophones play a cool swinging rhythm that feels something like bomp-do-bom-bomp. The form is interesting because it is a long section of music repeated twice.

0:00 | Verse 1A Domino plays a short descending piano part to start the song. Listen to the saxophones as they play their steady part behind Domino. In this section, the lyrics walk through the work week from Monday to Friday. Blue Monday. Hard Tuesday. On Wednesday, he's "beat to his socks" and Friday is payday!

0:43 | Bridge The rhythm changes in this part and it's pretty hard to miss. The drums, piano, bass, and guitar all start playing the same triplet rhythm that the piano had in the verse. It gives a different sense of energy to this section, and because it continues to pound away it builds a sense of tension as the musical pitch of the chords rises. The lyrics in this bridge section talk about the fun he is having on a Saturday night, out on the town with his girlfriend. As I listen, I can almost feel the energy of the famous Bourbon Street in New Orleans—the sounds of all the jazz and R&B clubs spilling onto the street.

1:02 | Verse 1B I called this section 1B, because it repeats the music from verse 1A of the song, but with some changes. It is a continuation of that section both musically and lyrically. It is as if the Saturday night revelry of the bridge was just an interruption in this story.

1:20 | Verse 2A Saxophone Solo
We can hear in this section that the music repeats the 1A music, but instead of Domino retelling the story of the work week, we can now hear a fantastic saxophone solo from Herb Hardesty.

1:39 | Bridge The same musical shift as last time, and Domino's vocals reenter. I love that the lyrics about the tiring work week blues are replaced with a saxophone solo in 2A, but in the bridge we still have the celebration of the Saturday fun. It takes a song that is called "Blue Monday" and makes the actual experience of it more about Saturday night.

1:57 | Verse 2B The same as 1B

JOHNNY CASH

Played: ROCK AND ROLL/COUNTRY

Known for his music as well as his famous "man in black" outlaw image, Johnny Cash (1932–2003) is one of the most iconic musicians of the twentieth century. The sound of Cash's music is a beautiful harmony of contradictions. He sang of murder and redemption, love and loss, war and hope. All of it was delivered in his signature deep bass voice, typically supported by a sparse arrangement. The majority of his early recordings, such as "Cry, Cry, Cry," feature Cash singing and playing guitar backed up by his group, the Tennessee Two—Luther Perkins on guitar and Marshall Grant on bass.

In 1968, he married his second wife, June Carter, whom he had loved for years. June was practically from country music royalty; her mother was none other than "Mother" Maybelle Carter, who helped to set the foundation of American roots music. Johnny and June's marriage led to a number of great musical unions in songs like "Jackson" and "It Ain't Me, Babe." They both died in 2003 in the middle of Johnny's comeback success with his cover of the Nine Inch Nails song "Hurt."

- PLAYLIST -

"Cry, Cry, Cry" (1955)

"Folsom Prison Blues" (1955)

"I Walk the Line" (1956)

"Get Rhythm" (1956)

"Ring of Fire" (1963)

"Orange Blossom Special" (1965)

"Jackson" with June Carter Cash (1967)

"Man in Black" (1971)

"I've Been Everywhere" (1996)

"Hurt" (2003)

HISTORICAL FACT/ SOCIAL CONNECTIONS

Cash was known as the man in black, for the black suit he wore, and many people associated it with his bad boy image. But as he said in his 1971 song "Man in Black," he wore that color to remind everyone that there were still evils in the world that needed to be abolished, such as poverty, racism, war, and hatred.

SONG FACTS: "RING OF FIRE" (1963)

Written by June Carter Cash and Merle Kilgore
Released on Columbia Records, April 1963

Since this is my book, I get to say things like, "This is one of the best songs ever." I'll admit it, I listened to Johnny Cash when I was young and I wanted to play guitar and dress in black—but even after all these years, I still think this is one of the most perfect songs ever recorded. While the music sounds fun and upbeat, the lyrics talk about the burning emotions that are stirred by falling into love with someone for the first time. Love is a fire that is out of control, and the deeper you fall, the more it burns. But the lyrics never talk about trying to get out of the fire, only about falling into the flames—isn't that the truth.

Johnny Cash and June Carter Cash

Sam Phillips and Johnny Cash

DESTINATIONS

Sun Records in Memphis, TN

Sun Records is still standing in the same location where Johnny Cash, Elvis Presley, and the rest recorded their great songs, at 706 Union Avenue in downtown Memphis, Tennessee. You can take a tour of the studio, and then when you're done you can walk just the few blocks to Beale Street—the famous street that was filled with blues singers in the 1940s and led Sam Phillips to Memphis in the first place. Beale Street is a bit more commercial these days, but you can still hear some great music and have some excellent barbecue.

"RING OF FIRE"

The music of this song is simple but potent. The basic rhythm is played by the drums, acoustic guitar, and acoustic bass. These three instruments keep the basic pulse all the way through. In the opening, we can hear mariachi-style trumpets playing. When June Carter Cash wrote the song, it was originally recorded by her sister Anita. Six months later when Johnny went to record it, he mentioned that the only thing it needed was the addition of those trumpets—and boy oh boy do they work great. The other major musical element is the backing vocals that are sung by June and the Carter sisters along with Maybelle Carter.

0:00 | Instrumental Introduction The mariachi horns dominate the opening of the song and set the mood. Behind the horns, we can hear the classic Cash instrumentation of guitar, bass, and drums.

0:09 | Verse 1 Listen to how Cash's voice and the trumpets work in a pattern known as call and response. For each line he sings, they respond back. The whole verse is based on playing a G major chord with an occasional move to C.

0:32 | Chorus The energy changes: The chord changes for the first time to a D. Johnny's voice jumps up into a higher register and we feel him projecting more energy. The backing vocals featuring June and the Carter sisters enter. In my mind, I always heard the almost angelic voices of the three-part close harmony as a perfect contradiction to Johnny's deep bass voice singing about falling into the deep flames. The melody does something really interesting here. As Cash sings the words, "down, down, down" the melody he is singing is made up of notes that are actually going up, up, up—so that, musically, the pitches represent our emotion (the excitement of new love), and not the direction he says he is falling.

0:50 | Instrumental An almost exact repeat of the opening of the song

1:06 | Chorus 2 Notice that Cash does not sing a second verse right here as we might expect but, instead, moves right back into the chorus. This time, in the chorus, listen to how when Cash sings the line "burns, burns, burns" the chord progression of the chorus stalls out. Again there is a bit of word painting, so that the song tells us we are stuck in the flames of love and there is nothing we can do about it.

1:23 | Verse 2 Finally, we get the second verse, that is the same as the first, but with new lyrics.

1:46 | Chorus 3

2:04 | Chorus 4 This last chorus adds some extra buildup and instrumentation to make it sound different and move to a conclusion. Eventually, it settles into a repetition of the song's title and begins to fade out.

THE SHIRELLES

Played: **ROCK AND ROLL/DOO-WOP**

- ⚡ PLAYLIST ⚡ -

"I Met Him on a Sunday" (1958)

"Dedicated to the One I Love" (1959)

"Tonight's the Night" (1960)

"Will You Love Me Tomorrow" (1960)

"Mama Said" (1961)

"Baby It's You" (1961)

"Soldier Boy" (1962)

"Everybody Loves a Lover" (1962)

"Foolish Little Girl" (1963)

"It's a Mad, Mad, Mad, Mad World" (1963)

The Shirelles started in 1957 when four teenage girls formed a singing group at their high school in Passaic, New Jersey. Shirley Owens (later Alston-Reeves), Doris Coley, Addie Harris, and Beverly Lee are often credited as being the first rock and roll girl group. What makes their story so interesting is that they were signed to a recording contract by Florence Greenberg, a mother of one of their classmates. Greenberg had no experience in the music industry and started her own record label called Tiara Records. In 1959, she renamed the label Scepter, and the Shirelles career really took off. The vocal harmony sung by the four girls was backed with lush arrangements featuring string instruments. Greenberg enlisted songwriter/producer Luther Dixon to help write and record songs like "Soldier Boy" and "Tonight's the Night."

Gerry Goffin and Carole King, circa 1959

HISTORICAL FACT/SOCIAL CONNECTIONS

By the late 1950s, the first wave of rock and roll was over, and singers like Elvis, Jerry Lee Lewis, Little Richard, and Chuck Berry all stopped recording for one reason or another (although all of them picked it up again in a few years). Suddenly, a number of new regional sounds rushed in to fill the gap, including the sounds recorded by independent record labels in New York. These labels hired songwriting teams who worked in music publishing houses located in New York City—including the famed Brill Building at 1619 Broadway. Many of these songwriters were teenagers who worked nine to five turning out hit songs for new groups. Some of the more famous songwriting teams were Carole King and Gerry Goffin, Jeff Barry and Ellie Greenwich, and Barry Mann and Cynthia Weil. The musical sound that developed became the essence of the girl groups—female vocal groups performing songs by Brill Building songwriters and produced by men like Luther Dixon or Phil Spector.

SONG FACTS: "WILL YOU LOVE ME TOMORROW" (1960)

Written by Gerry Goffin and Carole King
Released on Scepter Records, November 1960

This song is a great example of how the music industry in New York City worked at the start of the 1960s. Gerry Goffin and Carole King (who were married to each other) worked for the music publishing company Aldon Music that was owned by music mogul Don Kirshner. He asked them to write a song for the Shirelles that would serve as a follow-up to their song "Tonight's the Night." King wrote the music and Goffin wrote the lyrics, and soon enough, producer Luther Dixon was recording the song for Scepter Records.

TRY THIS AT HOME

Florence Greenberg

Florence Greenberg, the Shirelles, and even the Brill Building songwriters all learned the business side of the music industry while they were making hit records. Why don't you have some fun with this idea in your house? How could you manage your own music business? Things would be very different today from the way it was done in the 1960s. Now, we have the ability to record music on a computer at home, create a website for the label, and even market it on Facebook and Twitter. But first things first—what are you going to call the label? What kind of music do you want to sell? How will you reach your fans? Everyone in the family needs a job, so pick yours before someone else does.

"WILL YOU LOVE ME TOMORROW"

LISTENING GUIDE

Popular songs from this era often sound catchy and simple, but they are carefully crafted with a lot of depth and style. The voices of the Shirelles drift above a beautifully arranged background that changes as the song goes along. The form of this song follows the classic Tin Pan Alley song format of AABA—where A is a repeated section of music and the B is a new contrasting section. There is no separate chorus section in this song.

0:00 | Verse 1A This section of music is the foundation of the song, so we call it the "A section." Listen to what the various instruments are doing. You can hear a guitar strumming chords and a second guitar playing the "bop-di-bop, bop" rhythm along with the piano and percussion instruments. A bass guitar holds down the low end of the song. Listen to the simple but great vocal melody sung by Shirley, and then the rest of the group joins her for the second half of the verse. The section ends with a refrain, the line, "Will you still love me tomorrow?"

0:36 | Verse 2A Formally this section is a repetition of the first verse, so we can also call this a second A section. But listen carefully—can you hear how the arrangement expands the song? It adds string instruments playing along with the vocals. The background singers sing throughout the entire section. It once again ends with the refrain.

1:04 | Bridge B This is a section of new music and, as such, we can call it the "B section." The melody and the chord progression changes, but the rhythm instruments stay the same. The new string melody really steals the show here. Notice that it does not end with the refrain.

1:32 | Verse 3A After the contrasting B section, we have a return to the full A section.

2:00 | Verse 4A In the final A section, the strings play the main melody, and the singers only enter for the final refrain to close out the song.

2:28 | The refrain repeats to end the song in a fade out.

FRANKIE LYMON
AND THE TEENAGERS

Played: **ROCK AND ROLL / DOO-WOP**

-= PLAYLIST =-

"Why Do Fools Fall in Love" (1956)

"I Want You to Be My Girl" (1956)

"I Promise to Remember" (1956)

"The ABC's of Love" (1956)

"I'm Not a Juvenile Delinquent" (1957)

"Baby, Baby" (1957)

"Teenage Love" (1957)

"Love Is a Clown" (1957)

"Little Bitty Pretty One" (1960)

"I Put the Bomp" (1961)

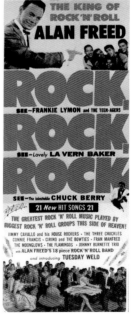

Poster for the film Rock, Rock, Rock!

For a group that wasn't together for very long, Frankie Lymon and the Teenagers had a tremendous influence on an entire generation of musicians. Their music helped to cement vocal harmony as a key ingredient of early rock and roll and even led to the development of what was later called Doo-Wop. The Teenagers were formed in New York City, and they quickly found an audience who loved their sweet vocal sounds and the high-pitched lead voice of Frankie Lymon. In 1956 and 1957 the group recorded a series of hit songs and planted the seeds for the rise of the boy bands. Frankie Lymon and the Teenagers not only recorded hits, but they also performed live and appeared on television and in movies. That same marketing blueprint is still being used in the early twenty-first century with groups like One Direction.

HISTORICAL FACT/SOCIAL CONNECTIONS

In 1951, Cleveland-based DJ Alan Freed was one of the first people to use the phrase "rock and roll" to describe the music he was playing on the radio. Most of what he played on the AM station 850 WJW was rhythm and blues that had what he called "the big beat." In 1954, he moved to New York City where he began to broadcast on WINS. Freed's show helped to bring artists like Frankie Lymon and the Teenagers to national prominence, and Freed even cast a number of these artists in the rock and roll films he made. In the 1956 film *Rock, Rock Rock!*, Frankie Lymon and the Teenagers performed two of their hit songs, "Baby Baby" and "I'm Not a Juvenile Delinquent." In these performances, you can also see their choreography and dancing. Think about how important it would have been for performers, especially for African Americans, to be featured in a movie that would be shown around the country to teenagers who were newly obsessed with the sound of rock and roll.

Written by Frankie Lymon
Released on Gee Records, January 1956

New York's Paramount Theater

This is the song that made Frankie Lymon and the Teenagers stars. Go online and take a look at their first national television appearance on the Frankie Laine show in New York from 1956 where they perform "Why Do Fools Fall In Love." Laine's introduction gives a great historical sense of the state of rock and roll at the time, and the song shows how dynamic the group was as performers (and, again, the dancing).

TRY THIS AT HOME

Vocal harmony was extremely popular in the 1950s and '60s among teens, who formed their own singing groups to perform on street corners and at high school dances. Many musicians started by singing with their family—give it a try and form your own group. Give everyone a different part to sing and perform a song together. Remember that doo-wop is often based on nonsense words and sounds, so make up your own bass part that goes "bomp-bomp-doo" and a rhythm part that goes, "chick-a-chick ow." Put them together and you have your own vocal arrangement.

LISTENING GUIDE

"WHY DO FOOLS FALL IN LOVE"

The musical form of this song is similar to the Shirelles "Will You Love Me Tomorrow," except that the whole structure goes by twice as fast and then repeats, with a saxophone solo added into the middle to vary the sound. Overall, it looks like this: Intro, AABA, Solo, AABAA. While many early rock and roll songs used a standard blues chord progression, early vocal harmony–based songs use an expanded harmonic vocabulary (often adding a minor chord built on the sixth scale degree).

0:00 | Introduction The bass singer, Sherman Garnes, begins the song with a rhythmic scat that will become the basic rhythm of the entire song. Lymon and the other vocalists enter at the same time as the drums singing "oooo, waa, oooo, waah." Notice that the drums play a steady backbeat throughout the entire song. This section ends with the refrain, "Why do fools fall in love."

0:15 | Verse 1 The song settles into a mid-tempo groove as the saxophone, electric guitar, and drums build the base for the singers to work over. Pay careful attention to the sound of the teenagers singing background. They are actually using a combination of nonsense syllables, words from the song, and extended ohhs and ahhs to make the rest of the musical sounds. It almost sounds like there are a large number of horns playing, but most of it is them. This section ends with the refrain, "Why do fools fall in love."

0:26 | Verse 2 New words, but almost the same music as verse 1.

0:37 | Bridge It is easy to hear the change into this part of the song. Both the chords and the melody change, and the backing vocalists stop singing, their cascading horn sounds, and switch to longer held tones.

0:48 | Verse 3 As the song comes back into the verse, Frankie pushes his voice into a soft melisma on the word "why" instead of singing a new set of lyrics. What a great musical idea. We can almost hear his young heart breaking, his soft voice pleading in a manner we haven't heard yet in the song. He ends the section with, "Tell me why."

0:59 | Saxophone solo
This might be the solo section for the saxophone, but all three instruments get a turn to take center stage. Listen carefully for the rhythmic repetition of the electric guitar chords (it's one of the first times you can hear the guitar clearly in the whole song). The drummer really pushes heavily on the backbeat in this section, which helps to build up the energy even though the voices are gone.

1:22 | Verse 4
1:33 | Verse 5
1:44 | Bridge
1:55 | Verse 6

2:06 | Extended Refrain to end the song
The final refrain of verse 6 is extended, which allows Frankie to move back into the soft falsetto he used in verse 3, and once again we feel the emotion as the song ends. The whole group gets to harmonize on a final longer version of the song's refrain to end the song.

THE BEATLES

Played: **ROCK AND ROLL/ROCK**

PLAYLIST

"Love Me Do" (1962)

"I Want to Hold Your Hand" (1963)

"Can't Buy Me Love" (1964)

"A Hard Day's Night" (1964)

"Help!" (1965)

"Yesterday" (1965)

"Yellow Submarine" (1966)

"All You Need is Love" (1967)

"Lucy in the Sky with Diamonds" (1967)

"Hey Jude" (1968)

"Revolution" (1968)

"Get Back" (1969)

"Let It Be" (1969)

The Beatles perform live on the Ed Sullivan Show, *February 9, 1964.*

The Beatles managed to transcend their original time and place (the 1960s in Liverpool) and become part of pop culture around the world. Because of this, it is often hard to believe that all the music the Beatles ever recorded as a group comes from a seven-year period between 1962 and 1969. The band consisted of the "Fab Four," (shown left to right) Paul McCartney (vocals and bass), George Harrison (vocals and guitar), Ringo Starr (sometimes vocals but mostly just drums) and John Lennon (vocals and guitar). There are a few key elements that made the Beatles great. They wrote and performed their own songs—in fact, John and Paul are often considered two of the greatest songwriters of the twentieth century. They were excellent musicians—their performances have artistry, and they sang in three-part harmony. They worked with a great producer—George Martin produced almost every Beatles album and helped to shape the overall sound.

HISTORICAL FACT/SOCIAL CONNECTIONS

The Beatles were at the forefront of the British Invasion, but it is important to remember that the invasion was firmly rooted in American music. This is a great way for your family to have a conversation about how music and culture move around the world. The story starts with American records coming to the United Kingdom in the late 1950s. Musicians then mixed the sound of rock and roll with local styles, such as skiffle and dance hall, and what resulted was a particularly British form of rock and roll. When the Beatles brought that sound to the United States, it became the new craze. Ask your family to think about how music travels around the world today. How is it different from the 1960s?

SONG FACTS: "I WANT TO HOLD YOUR HAND" (1963)

Written by John Lennon and Paul McCartney

Released on Parlophone (UK) and Capitol (US), November/December 1963

Recorded at EMI Studios, London, in October of 1963, this song is the perfect example of how the Beatles crafted their music. The early songs written by Lennon and McCartney used all the best little arts and pieces from the music they'd been playing in nightclubs for several years: girl groups, Motown, rock and roll, rhythm and blues. This song mixes these sounds together but also gives them a youthful spin. When the Beatles came to the United States in February of 1964 and performed this song on the Ed Sullivan show, they became superstars and this song rocketed to the top of the charts.

TRY THIS AT HOME

This is a good activity to try on a cold winter weekend when you can stay inside and watch a whole box of Beatles movies. They are important historical documents that let us see the Beatles at different times in their career, but they are also really good movies. The perfect two to watch is *A Hard Day's Night* (1964), *Help!* (1965), and the animated *Yellow Submarine* (1968). And if you have older kids and want to delve deeper into the history, then I recommend the multipart *The Beatles* anthology boxed set from 1996. The eight episodes walk you through their music using historic interviews, historic performance footage, and photos. [It]'s also a great way to see how the band's history related to what was happening during the 1960s.

LISTENING GUIDE

"I WANT TO HOLD YOUR HAND"

This is another song that uses the ABBA song formula, except the Beatles add an actual chorus after the refrain to extend the section. The overall structure looks like this: A (+Chorus), A (+Chorus), B, A (+Chorus), A (+Chorus). This song has a level of sophistication in its harmonic vocabulary that was new to rock and roll at the time, yet overall the song is simple and to the point. The song is in the key of G, and the chord progression adds to the basic blues chords.

0:00 | Introduction The song begins with a simple announcement, a three-note pattern repeated three times, and then a rhythmic buildup as the music stalls on that last note.

0:09 | Verse 1A Listen closely to the rhythm of the song, and you will notice the great rhythm created by the guitar and bass. Ringo holds down a steady beat on the drum kit and uses the open hi-hat cymbals to create a very active sound. The classic handclap pattern is almost like a rhythmic singalong; you just have to join in!

The verse of this song is in G major and plays using four chords: G major, D7, E minor, and B minor. It repeats that pattern except the second time it ends with a B major chord instead of the minor. It is a great way to create a subtle change of mood for the listener, from the sadness of the minor chord to the uplifting sound of the major. If we used the Roman numeral system of analysis to think about the relationship of these chords, we would have I, V7, vi, iii, and then I, V7, vi, and III. The section ends with a refrain on the words "I want to hold your hand" along with the B major chord.

0:23 | Chorus This section creates a full-fledged chorus for the song. The harmony uses mostly major chords: C major, D major, G major, and E minor for the first time they sing "I want to hold your hand," and then C major, D major, and then two measures of G major for the second time they say the words. Like the verse this creates melancholy the first time when it ends on a minor chord, and a sense of resolution when it ends on the tonic chord the second time. Using Roman numerals, it is IV, V, I, vi, V, IV, V, and I.

0:30 | Verse 2A

0:45 | Chorus

0:52 | Bridge B In classic AABA form, the B section changes to a new melody and harmonic progression, but it modulates to a new key: C major. The section uses the chords D minor, G major, C major, and A minor (which in the key of C is ii, V, I, and vi). The progression repeats and like the other sections of the song, the Beatles replace the final A minor with a major chord on the note D. This makes it a II chord in the key of C, but more importantly it is the V chord of the original key of G. This gives them a great way to push the song back into the verse after this diversion. The Beatles also change the mood of the music here to a much more introspective sound, just as the lyrics reflect on the narrator's emotions. The buildup back to the verse is reminiscent of the introduction.

1:12 | Verse 3A

1:27 | Chorus

1:34 | Bridge B

1:54 | Verse 4A Listen close for the great drum fill by Ringo at the end of the refrain.

2:10 | Chorus They add a new extension to finish the song.

THE ROLLING STONES

Played: **ROCK AND ROLL/ROCK**

~ PLAYLIST ~

"Come On" (1963)

"Time Is on My Side" (1964)

"(I Can't Get No) Satisfaction" (1965)

"Paint It Black" (1966)

"She's a Rainbow" (1967)

"Jumping Jack Flash" (1968)

"Sympathy for the Devil" (1969)

"Wild Horses" (1971)

"It's Only Rock and Roll" (1974)

"Miss You" (1978)

"Start Me Up" (1981)

"Rock and a Hard Place" (1989)

"Love Is Strong" (1994)

The Rolling Stones, 1964

Richards live on stage in 1978

The members of the Rolling Stones all came from the London area and bonded over their love for American R&B, rock and roll, and blues. They began by playing covers of that music in bars and clubs, calling themselves the Rolling Stones after the name of a Muddy Waters blues. When it came time to record their first record, they even chose to perform a cover of the Chuck Berry song, "Come On." If the Beatles had come to represent the acceptable image of a rock and roll band with their matching suits and haircuts, then the Rolling Stones would adopt the bad boy image—ruff, tuff, and ready to party. This image played into their songwriting, and many of the Stones' original compositions began to express the darker side of humanity (yes, there is talk of sex, drugs, and other things). For more than fifty years, they have been making music steeped in the traditions of American rock and roll.

HISTORICAL FACT/SOCIAL CONNECTIONS

When the bands of the British Invasion first hit the airwaves in the United States, it changed the face of popular music. Teens all across the country began listening to the new music, calling radio stations to request the songs, buying the albums in record-breaking numbers, watching the music on television, and going to see it at the movies. The music of the British Invasion began to eclipse much of the pre-1964 rock and roll by soul musicians, girl groups, and folk singers—only Motown was able to stand up to it on the charts.

Written by Mick Jagger and Keith Richards

Released on London (US) and Decca Records (UK), June/August 1965

This song has an excitement to it that has not faded over the years. I think it has to do with the opening guitar riff played by Keith Richards—one he claimed came to him in a dream, but also bears a striking resemblance to the horn part of Martha and the Vandellas' "Nowhere to Run" (1965). It's only three notes played with some fuzz box distortion to give the notes a ragged edge, but it grabs your attention right away with its attitude. Then there are the lyrics. We've all felt at one point in our lives that we couldn't be satisfied, that we were stuck in a rut. Mick Jagger takes this general feeling and connects it to the overall sense of angst that teenagers were feeling in the mid-1960s, and the rise of commercialism in society.

TRY THIS AT HOME

Jagger live on stage in 1999

Musical "labels" can be a funny thing. They can help us connect a number of songs that share a particular sound/style—like calling something funk music. They can help us talk about a mood created by the music—like sad songs. They can even help us identify music that comes from a particular time and place—like labeling something part of the British Invasion. But that last one is tricky, because even though a number of bands came out of England and made it big in the United States during the mid-1960s, they don't all sound alike. For example, take the Beatles and the Stones. They were both part of the British Invasion and may sound somewhat similar when compared to other styles of music. But if we simply use these kinds of distinctions, then we miss our chance to say how bands like the Stones and the Beatles are different. Go listen to some other British Invasion bands like the Kinks, the Who, the Animals, the Yardbirds, and the Hollies. Listen to the rhythm, melody, harmony, and instrumentation of each. What kinds of similarities and differences can you hear?

"(I CAN'T GET NO) SATISFACTION"

LISTENING GUIDE

I like to think of this song as a modern blues. It was the first great song written by Mick Jagger and Keith Richards, and much like the Beatles, they built their first songwriting attempts on the shoulders of the music they had been playing in clubs. The guitar part and tambourine sound like Motown, the vocals act like an old blues (but telling a modern story about all the things everyone else wants him to do), and the chorus sections feel like rock and roll. The form of the song is curious. It uses the basic verse/chorus model, but it plays with an unexpected structure.

0:00 | Introduction The classic guitar riff played by Keith Richards starts off the song. Then the rhythm section enters (drums and bass). Listen carefully to Bill Wyman's subtle bass playing. It doesn't draw attention to itself, but it creates a drive and bounce to the song.

0:15 | Chorus Mick Jagger's vocal enters as he sings the chorus of the song. Notice that the energy in this section actually feels like it is less than in the introduction. This is one of the strange things about the form of this song—the verses are the high point and the chorus is the mellow section. Think about it: How does this play into the song's statement that the singer "can't get no satisfaction"? The guitar plays a strummed pattern and not the riff. Try to clap along with the tambourine as it plays "1-2-3" on beats three and four of each measure. The song begins to build up energy with the repeated "I try and I try" vocals that get louder and more aggressive with each repetition.

0:42 | Verse 1 The opening riff returns, and the song shifts into the verse where the story is told. Jagger shouts over the guitar riff. This helps to portray the frustration the narrator feels, struggling to be heard over all the noise of the commercialism and useless information that he hears on the car radio. At the end of the verse, the song breaks with only the drums and tambourine continuing, and quickly pushes back into the chorus.

1:15 | Chorus
1:42 | Verse 2

2:15 | Chorus Listen carefully to the varied guitar playing by Keith Richards. It adds some new melodic ideas into the song.

2:44 | Verse

3:15 The verse is extended into a semichorus, using the riff to end.

THE SUPREMES

Played: **MOTOWN SOUL**

⸗ PLAYLIST ⸗

"Buttered Popcorn" (1961)

"Baby Love" (1964)

"Where Did Our Love Go" (1964)

"Come See About Me" (1964)

"Stop! In the Name of Love" (1964)

"I Hear a Symphony" (1965)

"You Can't Hurry Love" (1966)

"You Keep Me Hanging On" (1966)

"Reflections" (1967)

"Love Child" (1968)

"I'm Gonna Make You Love Me" (1968)

"Someday We'll Be Together" (1969)

The Supremes represent the pinnacle of the Motown Records label; they are also one of the only American groups that was able to compete with the sounds of the British Invasion on the *Billboard* charts. The group was formed by three high school girls who all grew up in the Brewster-Douglass housing projects of Detroit: Florence Ballard, Mary Wilson, and Diana Ross, shown left to right. They were inspired by the music and performance style of Frankie Lymon and the Teenagers, and were determined to get signed to the new Motown Records label located in Detroit and owned by Berry Gordy. They finally signed with Motown in 1961, and by 1964 they were one of the top singing groups in the world. After Ballard and Ross left the group, the Supremes continued to record until 1977 with a number of other singers including Cindy Birdson and Scherrie Payne.

HISTORICAL FACT/SOCIAL CONNECTIONS

The story of Motown Records is a remarkable one, not only for the way it came into being, and the way it was run as a business, but also for the staggering amount of talent that made music for them. The majority of records made in Detroit featured the same group of musicians playing on them—what we call session musicians. They called themselves The Funk Brothers and included Benny Benjamin, Eddie Brown, Joe Messina, Earl Van Dyke, and James Jamerson (whom I consider to be one of the best bass players of all time). Berry Gordy also employed a full-time staff of songwriters and arrangers including Norman Whitfield, Nick Ashford, Valerie Simpson, and even Smokey Robinson, whose talent and output rivaled the Brill Building system of New York.

Written by Holland-Dozier-Holland
Released on Motown Records, June 1964

The Supremes' big break came in 1964 when they began working with the songwriting team of Brian Holland, Lamont Dozier, and Eddie Holland (better known as Holland-Dozier-Holland). The partnership resulted in five number one singles in a row, and it all started with this song. In the early part of their career, the members of the Supremes would change who sang lead on each song, but once Diana Ross sang this song, she became the star of the group and the star of Motown.

DESTINATIONS

Motown Records, Detroit, MI, circa 1965

By 1972, Berry Gordy had fully moved the operations of Motown Records to Los Angeles, leaving its roots in Detroit behind. But the building that was called Hitsville, USA, is still standing and is now home to the Motown Museum. The museum includes various artifacts and exhibits, but the real treat is being able to stand in the actual Studio A—the very location where all the famous Motown hits were recorded.

LISTENING GUIDE

"WHERE DID OUR LOVE GO"

So far in this book we have looked at a number of musical forms including ones based on a verse/chorus structure, AABA, and even the twelve-bar blues. All of these are built on the idea of contrast between sections. But in a number of Motown tunes from the mid-1960s, the idea of contrast disappears and is replaced with a single idea (melody and chord progression) hammered home again and again with small nuances in the arrangements. If there is one thing to say about this era of Motown, it's hooks, hooks, and more hooks. Holland-Dozier-Holland wrote this song to immediately grab the listener's attention and never take a break from the action. It's two and a half minutes with no filler. As a footnote, I also have to mention the excellent cover of this song by Soft Cell; it's actually the second half of their song "Tainted Love" (1981).

0:00 | Rhythmic Introduction A short two-measure introduction sets up the basic rhythm for the entire song and includes the infectious handclaps (actually made by slapping pieces of wood together in the studio).

0:04 | Section 1 The first of ten eight-measure sections, this establishes a chord progression that will be used for the entire song. Use one chord per measure and play C, G, Dm7, G, and then a quick F to turn back around to the opening C. Repeat! For those of you still keeping track of the Roman numeral analysis, it's I, V, ii7, V (IV). Ross sings lead on the song. Her tone is soft but still projects a sense of power behind it. Pay attention to the repeated piano chords and thumping bass that support her voice.

0:18 | Section 2 New lyrics, but otherwise a melodic and harmonic repetition of section 1. Listen to how the arrangement is changed by adding ringing vibraphone, snare drum rhythm, and horns playing softly on the backbeat.

0:33 | Section 3 This time around, we get the addition of Ballard and Wilson singing "baby baby, where did our love go?" in the background.

0:47 | Section 4

1:01 | Section 5

1:05 | Section 6—saxophone solo A fun sax solo plays to the same chord progression but adds a new melody to break things up at the midpoint.

1:30 | Section 7 The song jumps right back to where it left off in section 5.

1:44 | Section 8

1:57 | Section 9 The band suddenly stops playing on the last two measures of the section, leaving only Ross, Ballard, and Wilson singing over the percussion from the introduction.

2:12 | Section 10 Again, the band stops on the last two measures.

2:26 | Section 11 The song fades out on the first four measures, but the song does not change. It sounds like it could go on forever, but we are turning away from it; I think this is one of the reasons it makes you want to listen again right away.

JAMES BROWN

Played: **RHYTHM AND BLUES/SOUL/FUNK**

— PLAYLIST —

"Please, Please, Please" (1956) as the Famous Flames

"Try Me" (1958) as James Brown and the Famous Flames

"Night Train" (1962)

"Papa's Got a Brand New Bag" (1965)

"I Got You (I Feel Good)" (1965)

"It's a Man's, Man's, Man's World" (1966)

"Cold Sweat" (1967)

"Say It Loud—I'm Black and I'm Proud" (1968)

"Funky Drummer" (1970)

"Super Bad (Parts 1 & 2)" (1970)

"Make It Funky" (1971)

"The Payback" (1974)

"Get Up Offa That Thing" (1976)

"Living in America" (1985)

James Brown dancing with Johnny Carson, 1967

James Brown (1933–2006) was called the "Godfather of Soul" for good reason. His long career saw him performing in a number of different musical styles, but they were linked together through his signature voice and powerful presence. In 1955, Brown joined Bobby Byrd's rhythm and blues vocal group, the Famous Flames, and quickly had a hit with the song "Please Please, Please." By the early 1960s, Brown had formed his own band (with many of the Flames still singing background), and by 1965 they were turning out a stream of hit songs that pushed into the territory of soul music; listen to "Papa's Got a Brand New Bag." The big transformation came in 1967 with the song "Cold Sweat," in which Brown and his band (featuring Pee Wee Ellis, Maceo Parker, Jimmy Nolen, Bernard Odum, and drummer Clyde Stubblefield) defined a new sound that would be called funk.

HISTORICAL FACT/SOCIAL CONNECTIONS

James Brown, the "Godfather of Soul," performs on the TV show Soul Train *in 1971.*

King Records was started in 1943 by Syd Nathan and was originally formed as a country music label with artists like Reno and Smiley. But the location in Cincinnati, Ohio (on the border with Kentucky and close to Indiana) eventually led to an interesting mix of rhythm and blues, country, and gospel artists all recording in the same place. It was also notable for being one of the first record labels to house the entire business—recording studios, offices, art department, pressing plant, packaging, and distribution—all in one building at 1540 Brewster Avenue. James Brown became the number one star of King Records and even a guiding musical force for the label in the 1960s.

SONG FACTS: "SUPER BAD, PARTS 1 & 2" (1970)

Written by James Brown
Released on King Records, October 1970

While Brown's song "Say It Loud—I'm Black and I'm Proud" may be the more obvious statement of black power in the United States during the late 1960s, you will quickly notice that "Super Bad" continues that message. Throughout the song Brown uses slang common in African American communities during the late 1960s, such as "right on" (a positive affirmation), and "super bad" (meaning totally awesome!). Within the song, Brown presents an image of himself as positive, powerful (with soul power), and as an educator. During the bridge section, he encouraging "brothers and sisters" to be true to themselves, or they won't know "what it's about." In this song, the rhythm and the message are both invigorating.

TRY THIS AT HOME

James Brown influenced many musicians who adopted his brand of soul-based funk music along with his energetic dance moves and stage antics. Have some fun and try to find the James Brown influence in music of the twenty-first century. Listen to Janelle Monáe's "Tightrope" from 2010. The funky rhythm section that grooves for extended sections and her rapid-fire spoken-sung vocal delivery. Now, go watch her music video. Hint: Everything she does in the hospital room at the start taken from him, as well as the later scene when she is dancing on the table in the mess hall.

"SUPER BAD, PARTS 1 & 2"

LISTENING GUIDE

"Super Bad" features Brown's early '70s band called the J.B.'s and includes a number of amazing musicians: Robert McCollough (saxophone), Bobby Byrd (organ), Catfish Collins (guitar), Bootsy Collins (bass), and John "Jabo" Starks (drums). The song features an almost static harmony, sitting on a D major chord for the first minute and a half. It finally changes to a G major chord in the bridge, with a short moment on A before moving back into the verse. Because of this, the focus moves to the rhythm and the interweaving melodic lines, a perfect example of how Brown and his band forged the sound of modern funk during the late 1960s. When we think of funk music, one thing in particular should come to mind—groove. How long is the groove in this song? If you listen closely, it is only about two measures, but that small bit of music is used to build most of the song.

0:00 | Introduction James counts off the band, and then demands the listener's attention as he shouts, "Watch me!" Of course, this could mean a lot of things. He could be telling the audience to watch his dance moves, the band to watch him as the bandleader, or even his contemporary listeners to watch him as an example of black pride.

0:19 | Verse 1 and Chorus Listen closely to how each instrument plays its own short musical idea. Nobody plays anything particularly elaborate, but each small idea works with all the others to make the whole. It's like the pieces of a puzzle that show the whole picture only when they all fit together.

0:42 | Verse 2 and Chorus Listen to how Catfish Collins varies the guitar part: a single-note melody in the verse, and scratchy strummed chords in the chorus.

1:04 | Verse 3 and Chorus Listen to Bootsy Collins's bass. He sinks deep into the groove with a bass line that never stops moving but always accents the main rhythm of the song.

1:35 | Bridge James shouts out "bridge," giving instruction to the band—and they slide into the new section. This part sounds like a monumental shift because the band has been sitting on the same musical notes and rhythms for the entire first minute and a half of the song. Now they shift from D to G and the horns blast out a new melody.

If anyone ever asks you to prove that Jabo Starks was one of the best drummers in rock and roll, you should just play them this section. The polyrhythm he is playing is quite complex, and just listen to that rhythm produced by the ride cymbal. James gives a shout and a "Squeeeiiiiiii!!!!" and it's back to the verse music.

2:27 | Sax Solo 1 This section uses the music of the verses but allows saxophonist Robert McCollough to solo.

2:42 | Verse 4 and Chorus

2:58 | Verse 5 and Chorus

3:20 | Bridge Back to the bridge music and the funky drumming.

4:01 | Sax Solo 2 A second solo from McCollough ends the song, and James tells us the spiritual inspiration for the solo when he says, "blow me some Trane brother"—referring of course to great jazz saxophonist John Coltrane.

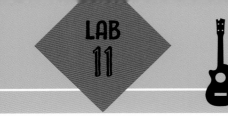

Played: **FOLK/ROCK**

Gerde's Folk City nightclub and restaurant, West 4th Street in Greenwich Village, New York City

Robert Zimmerman was born in 1941 in Duluth, Minnesota, and as a young man he was interested in music and poetry. By the time he walked into the folk revival music clubs of Greenwich Village, New York City in 1961, he had adopted the stage name Bob Dylan. He would soon become one of the most important figures in rock and roll history. Dylan wanted to create music that spoke to his listeners about the problems of the world and the concerns of everyday people. To accomplish this he merged poetic language, the immediacy of folk music, and the energy of rock and roll and built a new form of rock that talked about what was important—but still made you want to tap your feet and sing along. He has been actively recording and performing for more than fifty years.

HISTORICAL FACT/SOCIAL CONNECTIONS

The term folk music itself is rather vague, and it is often used along with other umbrella terms such as popular music and classical music. At its most basic, the term implies traditional music that has existed in a community for generations and is frequently performed by people in that community (= music of the people). When the term folk music is used in the case of someone like Bob Dylan, we are actually talking about the American folk-revival moment that began in the 1930s and reached its height of popularity in the 1960s. During the late 1950s and early 1960s, the folk-revival scene was booming in Greenwich Village, and clubs like Gerde's Folk City (where Dylan played his first professional gig), the Village Gate, and the Gaslight Coffee House drew crowds interested in listening that mingled with the performers.

SONG FACTS: "LIKE A ROLLING STONE" (1965)

Written by Bob Dylan | Released on Columbia Records, July 1965

According to Dylan, this song started as a ten-page poem he wrote in early 1965. He then recorded the song for inclusion on his sixth studio album, *Highway 61 Revisited*. But the performance of this song at the Newport Folk Festival on July 25, 1965, has become part of rock and

...ylan in 1978

...oll legend. It is known as the moment
...at Dylan "went electric." The crux of
...e story is that Dylan, by performing
...is song with the Paul Butterfield Blues
...and, had forsaken folk music in favor
...f rock and roll. But what many did not
...ealize at the time was that Dylan had
...one something else altogether. He had
...erged the social activism and political
...oncerns of folk with the sound and
...nergy of rock and roll music.

...RY THIS AT HOME

...ne of the things that attracted Dylan
... the folk music of Woody Guthrie and
...ete Seeger was the way the music
...lked about topical events, things that
...ere happening in the real world. To
...ylan, it was as if that music connected
... the communities and people it
...lked about, giving the common
...erson a voice in society in a way that
...ommercialized music could not. And
...e also liked the idea that anyone could
... involved as a performer. If the songs
...ere simple, then almost anyone who
...eard them could grab a guitar and learn
... play a few chords and sing along.
... are you feeling inspired? How about
...riting your own folk song lyrics about
...ur neighborhood or current events?

LISTENING GUIDE

"LIKE A ROLLING STONE"

At the time, this 6-minute song was too long for radio, too rock for folk, and too clever for rock—but in the end it changed everything as songwriters and musicians responded to Dylan's newfound sense of storytelling, political action, and extended rock sounds. Lyrically, the song talks about the way that material things can end up defining us and controlling our lives and how easily they can slip away. The song first mocks the character Little Miss Lonely (who had everything and lost it) for the way that she never cared about helping those with less, but at the end of the song, Dylan seems to suggest that she is now free from that materialism with a new world ahead of her.

0:00 | Instrumental Introduction The opening of this song is sonically dominated by Al Kooper's organ part.

0:11 | Verse 1 The song settles into a groove featuring drums, organ, piano, guitar, and bass. Listen carefully and you can hear some great playing on the "tack" piano in the background. Dylan begins to tell the tale of Little Miss Lonely and how she looked down on everyone.

1:00 | Chorus Dylan opens the chorus with the question, "Oh, how does it feel?"—talking directly to his main character. We can hear the emotion in his voice as he strains to hold out the high notes. Dylan's voice has a very particular timbre that is almost immediately recognizable. His vocal sound is thin and high, and his accent suggests a working-class singer (part of his folk music roots). The chorus ends with a short harmonica melody played by Dylan (again, part of the folk music tradition).

1:34 | Verse 2 Listen to how Dylan sings each musical phrase. He often rushes part of the lyrics/melody and then slows down on a particular note and holds it out for a long time.

2:24 | Chorus

3:02 | Verse 3

3:52 | Chorus Make sure to listen closely for the great organ part and the extended harmonica at the end.

4:30 | Verse 4

5:20 | Chorus and End Jam to Fadeout If you want to hear an interesting alternate early take of the song, go listen to the version on *Dylan's The Bootleg Series 1–3 (1961–1991)*.

Eric Clapton, 1975

CHAPTER 2:
⚡ ROCKING OUT ⚡

Jimmy Page, 1977

Played: **PSYCHEDELIC ROCK**

⟶ PLAYLIST ⟵

"Blues from an Airplane" (1966)

"Somebody to Love" (1967)

"White Rabbit" (1967)

"Embryonic Journey" (1967)

"Lather" (1968)

"Crown of Creation" (1968)

"Wooden Ships" (1969)

"Volunteers" (1969)

"When the Earth Moves Again" (1971)

"Long John Silver" (1972)

Jefferson Airplane at Webster Hall in New York City, 1967

Jefferson Airplane was one of the primary bands to develop psychedelic rock, a style that features longer songs with improvisational sections, new sounds created by electronic instruments, nontraditional rock instruments (e.g., sitar, harpsichord), and lyrics that use surrealistic imagery. Founder Marty Balin (guitar/vocals) started the group as the house band for his music club, the Matrix, located at 3138 Fillmore Street in San Francisco. Over the next two years he assembled an impressive list of musicians from the local scene, resulting in the classic lineup of the band that included Paul Kantner and Jorma Kaukonen (guitar/vocals), Jack Casady (bass), Spencer Dryden (drums), and Grace Slick (vocals). They were the first psychedelic band to reach a major level of success with their album *Surrealistic Pillow* (1967), but many of their friends soon followed including the Grateful Dead, Big Brother and the Holding Company, and the Quicksilver Messenger Service.

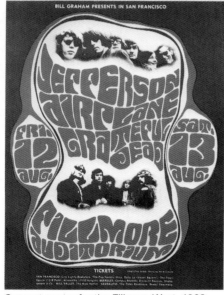

Concert poster for the Fillmore West, 1966

HISTORICAL FACT/SOCIAL CONNECTIONS

Hippies at the corner of Haight and Ashbury, 1967

Jefferson Airplane provides a great opportunity to look at the growth of the counterculture in the United States during the mid-1960s. The most obvious developments to talk about are the rise of communal living, the use of recreational drugs as a mind-altering experience, expanded musical sounds, and the turn to Eastern philosophy as a method of guiding your mind and soul into new ways of experiencing and understanding the world around you. The adults and teens in the family can explore the writings of the Beat poets/authors who were such a huge influence on the music of the counterculture (Ginsberg, Kerouac, Burroughs). For a somewhat fictionalized firsthand account of the scene and some of its central figures, check out Tom Wolfe's *The Electric Kool-Aid Acid Test* (1968).

The lyrics of the song are based on surrealistic images from Lewis Carroll's *Alice in Wonderland* books. There are many ways to interpret the dreamlike nature of the words. One way is to hear it as a straight reworking of the characters and images of the original books (a great way to listen with younger family members). The second, and more interesting way, is to connect the images to the shifting landscape of American society in 1967 (a conversation better suited for teens and adults in the family). Alice might represent someone lost in the upheaval of '60s society. Several references can be connected to the use of drugs within the counterculture ("one pill makes you larger," "some kind of mushroom") and the philosophy of expanding one's mind to new ways of thinking ("feed your head").

DESTINATIONS

Take a trip to the city by the bay on the West Coast of the United States, San Francisco. Many of the original buildings have changed, but you can still visit the historic neighborhoods. Visit the beautiful Golden Gate Park that hosted the Human Be-In event in early 1967 and helped set off the Summer of Love later that year. Bordering the park is the Haight-Ashbury district where many of the counterculture bands lived and performed.

LISTENING GUIDE

"WHITE RABBIT"

Jefferson Airplane sounds different from much of the music we looked at in chapter 1. They blended electrified blues guitar, strummed folk guitar, folk music–inspired poetic/political lyrics, and a sense of melody and song that drew from mid-'60s Beatles albums such as *Rubber Soul* (1965) and *Revolver* (1966). The musical form of "White Rabbit" is one continuous buildup. It is often compared to the structure of the 1928 composition Boléro by composer Maurice Ravel. "White Rabbit" approximates a traditional bolero rhythm in the bass and drum parts—listen for the repeating rhythmic pattern of two long notes followed by a series of shorter notes and a final long note.

0:00 | Instrumental Introduction The bass guitar establishes the basic bolero rhythm of the song (although this is counted in a 4/4 meter, as opposed to the typical 3/4 of bolero). The bass is quickly joined by the snare drum. The electric guitar enters playing a wandering melody that has a vaguely Spanish sound.

0:28 | Vocal Section Grace Slick enters singing the main melody. Listen to the timbre of her voice. For the most part, it is soft and wispy, but she also varies the volume of certain notes—pushing them forward in our soundscape. The electric guitar begins to play along with the other instruments using the same rhythm.

0:46 | Buildup This is the first of several sections when the music begins to build up and subtly push to a new level of activity and louder volume. The most obvious changes are that the electric guitar plays louder strummed chords, held out longer, and the bass guitar changes its melody for the first time since the opening of the song. Slick sings what can be heard as a bit of a refrain, "Go ask Alice . . ."

0:56 | Vocal Section 2 This vocal section is very similar to the last. While the general volume of the song has increased, the instruments return to their basic bolero rhythmic pattern. Slick's vocal performance has changed to a much stronger presentation. If you listen carefully, you will also notice that throughout the song she sounds like she is off in the distance—an effect created by the use of reverb in the studio.

1:13 | Buildup 2 The guitar and snare drum push harder and play louder on the main rhythm. Slick sings the refrain with slightly different words, "To call Alice . . ."

1:22 | Vocal Section 3—"the rock out" This section is the most dramatically different from the rest. The drummer switches from the rolled snare drum to a full drum kit and plays a typical 4/4 rock beat. The electric guitar strums forceful downstrokes on each beat. The bass moves to a walking bass pattern.

1:41 | Buildup 3 The drummer continues to play the full kit but returns to the bolero rhythm along with the bass. Again, Slick sings the refrain, "Go ask Alice . . ."

1:49 | Vocal Section 4 The music keeps the same intensity as the last buildup, and things are getting rather wild. Just for fun, one time you are listening to this section of the song, jump back to the start of the song. You might be amazed at how different it sounds and feels.

2:06 | Finale The band rocks out to the end while Slick shouts, "feed your head."

THE BYRDS

Played: **FOLK ROCK/PSYCHEDELIC ROCK/COUNTRY ROCK**

~ PLAYLIST ~

"Mr. Tambourine Man" (1965)

"I'll Feel a Whole Lot Better" (1965)

"Turn, Turn, Turn! (To Everything There Is a Season)" (1965)

"Set You Free This Time" (1965)

"Eight Miles High" (1966)

"So You Want to Be a Rock and Roll Star?" (1967)

"Wasn't Born to Follow" (1968)

"Space Odyssey" (1968)

"Hickory Wind" (1968)

"You Ain't Going Nowhere" (1968)

"Ballad of Easy Rider" (1969)

"Chestnut Mare" (1970)

The Byrds in 1965 (l to r: Hillman, Clark, McGuinn, Clarke, and Crosby)

The Byrds (1964–1973) were one of the most influential musical groups of the 1960s. Their earliest recordings show the immediate influence of two of the era's biggest artists: the Beatles and Bob Dylan. In fact, The Byrds often covered Dylan songs in a style that sounded like the Beatles, such as their first hit "Mr. Tambourine Man."

The lineup of the band changed several times over the years, and each time they experimented with a new musical approach. As a result, the group was part of originating three new rock styles: folk rock, psychedelic rock, and country rock. Throughout all of the changes, the group maintained its affinity for multipart harmony singing. The most prominent members of the group included Roger McGuinn (guitar), Gene Clark (guitar), David Crosby (guitar), Michael Clarke (drums), Chris Hillman (bass), and Gram Parsons (guitar).

The Byrds record vocals at Columbia Records Studios, 1965.

HISTORICAL FACT/SOCIAL CONNECTIONS

The Sunset Strip during the 1966 "hippie riots"

The Byrds provide an opportunity to look at the counterculture in Los Angeles, where the cultural and musical scene was quite different from San Francisco— for example, LA was home to the garage rock sound. Hollywood and the Sunset Strip, in particular, were the focus for the countercultural scene early on and were the location of the so-called "hippie riots" of 1966 that are the subject of the Buffalo Springfield song "For What It's Worth." Remember that, while many of the original concepts of the counterculture were adopted to break free from the previous generation and mainstream society, many of these ideas became diluted and misrepresented as they reached a wider audience and even led to the rise of the classic rock cliché, "sex, drugs, and rock and roll."

SONG FACTS: "EIGHT MILES HIGH" (1966)

Written by Gene Clark, Roger McGuinn, David Crosby

Released on Columbia Records, March 1966

This song is an important connection between the songwriting concepts of folk rock and the experimentation of psychedelic rock. It is often considered to be the first psychedelic rock song due to its use of impressionistic lyrics and modal jazz influences. The lyrics evoke strange imagery such as the "rain grey town known for its sound." Like "White Rabbit," it is possible to look at these lyrics from multiple perspectives. One way is to connect them to an actual trip the Byrds took to England around the time they wrote the song. Many in 1966 saw these lyrics as a not-so-subtle reference to drug use captured in the song's title. The truth most likely lies somewhere between the two.

DESTINATIONS

The Byrds got their start on the Sunset Strip in Los Angeles. Though many of the clubs have changed names and owners, you can still check out the scene there today. The official strip is about a mile and a half of Sunset Boulevard between Crescent Heights Boulevard and Doheny Drive that contains many of the famous rock clubs like the Roxy and the Whisky a Go Go. Before your visit make sure to enjoy the 1967 teen movie *Riot on Sunset Strip* that features the song "Riot on Sunset Strip" by the garage rock band the Standells.

LISTENING GUIDE

"EIGHT MILES HIGH"

Musically, the Byrds experimented with multiple guitar and vocal parts that weaved sounds together to form a unique musical texture. The song is only 3 minutes and 35 seconds long, but it always feels to me like it pushes at the boundaries of that time. The music was influenced by the sounds of Indian classical music, in which there is a slow unfolding of musical ideas based on a particular melodic or rhythmic idea (called a raga), and the modal/free jazz of musicians like John Coltrane, who showed an affinity for drones (a long, sustained tone) and ostinatos (consistently repeated patterns). Both of these ideas give the music a static character that features short-term repetition creating long-form structure.

0:00 | Instrumental Introduction The bass guitar establishes a simple repetitive melody and the galloping rhythm of the song.

The drums enter with a heavily syncopated beat. Listen carefully for the shifting accents on the cymbals and the tom-toms.

The electric guitar passage has a vaguely "Eastern" sound to it, and is reminiscent of the nontonal music of free jazz (without a tonal center or central note).

All of these musical parts work together to form a kind of musical quilt in which each piece builds a portion of the overall sound, but none of them is directly tied to the others.

0:29 | Verse 1 This is the only time the phrase "Eight miles high" is uttered since the lyrics of the song are through-composed (meaning it is written as a continuing thought with no repetition).

Notice that the music falls into a more traditional rock and roll format during this section. The drums turn to a classic 4/4 with a backbeat while the bass and guitar play a folk music–inspired chord progression.

1:00 | Verse 2 During this verse, try to focus on the detailed musical harmonies created by the different vocal parts. The main melody of the song often stays in one musical range, with only small movements in pitch, and then jumps to a different higher range. Each voice sings a slightly different version of the melody to create a lush hypnotic effect.

1:33 | Instrumental Break The more structured elements of the verses begin to drop away quickly and each instrument returns to the unique sonic creation we heard in the introduction.

This time, the guitar takes an extended solo played by Roger McGuinn. The unique timbre of the solo is achieved by using a twelve-string guitar.

2:22 | Verse 3

2:51 | Instrumental Break 2 Another wild solo is featured in the final section of the song. It frequently plays the notes of the opening guitar solo melody, thus creating a sense of closure. The song ends with all the instruments playing a strummed eighth-note rhythm.

LED ZEPPELIN

Played: **HARD ROCK**

⌐ PLAYLIST ⌐

"Good Times Bad Times" (1969)

"Whole Lotta Love" (1969)

"Heartbreaker" (1969)

"Immigrant Song" (1970)

"Rock and Roll" (1971)

"Stairway to Heaven" (1971)

"Dancing Days" (1973)

"Kashmir" (1975)

"Achilles Last Stand" (1976)

"In the Evening" (1979)

"Fool in the Rain" (1979)

Led Zeppelin, 1969 (l to r: Jones, Plant, Bonham, Page)

Formed in England in 1968, Led Zeppelin may be one of the most recognizable of all classic rock bands, both for their sound and image. After the Beatles established the iconic image of the four-person rock band in the 1960s, Zeppelin updated it for the '70s as a hard-rocking group with a sense of mystery and attitude

Most journalists, historians, and fans agree that Led Zeppelin is the beginning of the hard rock sound and the grandfather of heavy metal. All of this from a band that got its name from the fact that the drummer of the Who, Keith Moon, told them that the band was going to crash like a lead zeppelin.

Jimmy Page

HISTORICAL FACT/SOCIAL CONNECTIONS

Their music was powerful, yet often subtle, and this is a real testament to the talent of the four musicians in the band. Jimmy Page was already an established guitarist when he helped form Zeppelin out of the ashes of his last band, the Yardbirds. Robert Plant sang with a voice that ranged from breathy quiet whispers to howling animalistic screams. Bassist John Paul Jones held down the bottom end with a steady bass sound, but his talent as an arranger and keyboard player really came out on the later albums. And then there is the late, great John Bonham, whose heavy-handed fast drumming never lost the groove and set the standard for so many other rock drummers to follow.

Robert Plant, 1977

Written by Jimmy Page and Robert Plant

Released on Atlantic Records, November 1971

I think a word has to be said here about the prominence and legend of this song in rock history. Over the years, the song has either been the height of cool—as when the original HBO TV show version of the song "Tribute" (1999) by Tenacious D made it clear that "Stairway to Heaven" was actually the "greatest and best song in the world"—or it has been the height of overindulgence and the past—as when the film *Wayne's World* (1992) featured a guitar shop with a sign that read "No Stairway to Heaven," a joke about how overplayed the song was by classic rock radio and budding guitar players. On any one album, Zeppelin could rock out, blaze classic blues riffs, or perform a quiet ballad, and while there are plenty of great Zeppelin songs to choose from, "Stairway" covers all the bases.

TRY THIS AT HOME

While the members of Led Zeppelin were inspired by early rock and roll and its roots, they also were part of a generation for whom the music of the psychedelic '60s was a large influence. Surreal imagery and "far-out" ideas were the normal, and many songwriters of the time turned to literature for inspiration. For example, Zeppelin has at least three songs that make reference to, or draw inspiration from, J. R. R. Tolkien's *The Hobbit*: "Ramble On," "Misty Mountain Hop," and "The Battle of Evermore." So, what kind of literature-inspired rock song are you going to write? Will it be a ballad based on Stephenie Meyer's *Twilight* series? How about a scary tune based on the work of Stephen King? Or even take inspiration from Led Zeppelin and update their idea—write a series of tunes about Harry Potter ("The Battle of Hogwarts" anyone?).

LISTENING GUIDE

"STAIRWAY TO HEAVEN"

At just over 8 minutes and containing four distinct sections of music, "Stairway to Heaven" is an epic song. The changing arrangement helps to paint a picture as it grows and crescendos. The lyrics are pretty abstract, we can layer different meanings onto it, but the song involves a woman who believes that her love of material things can buy her salvation, which the song suggests is not true. Because the song is long and fairly detailed, focus on the large-scale structure.

0:00 | Opening Acoustic Section Plucked acoustic guitar and recorders open the song. The recorder is a flutelike British instrument that dates back to medieval times and gives the song a feeling of starting, a long time ago. Listen to how Plant's voice rises and falls in pitch and volume, sometimes high and loud, and at other times low and soft.

2:15 | Electric Section For the first time, things take a dramatic step as the strummed guitar opens up a new world of sound—electric instrumentation. We now can hear electric guitars and a Rhodes digital piano (playing the bass part). There are still recorders in the background playing a countermelody to Plant's vocals. The percussion finally enters the song with a drum fill at 4:15 (!), and brings with it a sense of urgency that the song is really moving ahead. The bass guitar also enters with its own melody.

5:33 | Guitar Solo Frequently voted one of the best guitar solos in rock history, it receives a proper introduction in the music as the song pauses, then announces the new section like trumpet calls from the castle gates. Listen to the timbre of Jimmy Page's guitar. It has a touch of distortion on it, giving it an edge, but the tone is also clear, allowing us to hear every bend and fingering.

6:45 | Hard Rock Section The song's climactic section lasts only one minute but is a full-out hard rock song with chugging rhythms (listen to the bass, drums, and guitar rhythm between each of the lyric lines), full-out vocals from Plant (compare it to the sound of his voice at the start), and electric guitar melodies in the background (listen carefully).

7:45 | Vocal Ending As if to remind us what the song was all about, they end it with a short, soft vocal phrase from Plant, "and she's buying a stairway to heaven."

JIMI HENDRIX

Played: **PSYCHEDELIC ROCK/HARD ROCK**

⌐ PLAYLIST ⌐

"Foxy Lady" (1967)

"Purple Haze" (1967)

"Manic Depression" (1967)

"Hey Joe" (1967)

"Fire" (1967)

"Spanish Castle Magic" (1967)

"Little Wing" (1967)

"Bold as Love" (1967)

"Crosstown Traffic" (1968)

"Voodoo Chile (A Slight Return)" (1968)

"All Along the Watchtower" (1968)

The life and career of Jimi Hendrix (1942–1970) were remarkable and somewhat sad. Born and raised in Seattle, he began to play the guitar in his teens and quickly picked up on the sound of classic blues guitarists like Howlin' Wolf, rock and roll guitarists like Duane Eddy, and the songs of Elvis. After a short stint in the army, he found himself performing on the chitlin' circuit as a member of the backing band for some of the great black musicians of the early 1960s including Wilson Pickett, the Isley Brothers, and even Little Richard. In a strange twist of fate, it was British musician Chas Chandler of the Animals who first recognized what an incredible talent Hendrix was and brought him over to England, where

Jimi Hendrix performs at the Monterey Pop Festival, 1967

he formed a band called the Jimi Hendrix Experience. After some success in the United Kingdom, the band came to the United States in 1967 to support their first album, and was introduced on the stage of the Monterey Pop Festival by Rolling Stones member Brian Jones. This performance ended with Hendrix lighting his guitar on fire in what has now become an iconic image in rock history—and shortly after catapulted him into worldwide fame.

Hendrix, 1969

SONG FACTS: "PURPLE HAZE" (1967)

Written by Jimi Hendrix

Released on Track Records, May 1967

After only four years of prolific musical output (1967–1970), Hendrix was dead. We had only begun to see the genius of this young man who was looking to expand his musical sound more and more everyday. Who knows what he would have done next had he lived, but undeniably he left some great music behind. "Purple Haze" represents one of his great guitar masterpieces. It pulls together many of the various techniques he'd been working on—jazz-influenced chords, the use of effects pedals to change the sound of the guitar, and the use of riffs to build the structure—and it puts them all into a great song with a catchy melody. While many at the time heard the lyrics as a drug reference (much like the Byrds' "Eight Miles High"), Hendrix often said it was actually just a love song as evidenced by the line, "that girl put a spell on me."

DESTINATIONS

The Bethel Woods Center for the Arts

Visit the location of the original Woodstock Music and Arts Festival where Hendrix performed in 1969. The event actually took place in Bethel, New York. The Bethel Woods Center for the Arts is located on the same spot and is now home to the Museum at Bethel Woods, where you can experience exhibits about the historic site and the history of the 1960s. You can also travel to the nearby village of Woodstock and spend time in the shops and restaurants. This part of upstate New York is particularly beautiful in the spring and fall.

LISTENING GUIDE

"PURPLE HAZE"

Try to focus on the sound of Hendrix's guitar throughout the song, and see if you can hear all the different tones he is able to create.

0:00 | Instrumental Introduction This is a powerful opening. The guitar announces itself by playing an octave interval. There is an effect on the guitar that also adds the same notes he is playing an octave below, so what he hear is an octave interval moving up and down an octave.

At 7 seconds a solo-style riff enters that will return, and it also serves as the basis for many of the licks we hear in the song.

0:33 | Verse 1 The strummed electric guitar chords repeat behind the vocal. The drums take a powerful fill after each lyrical phrase. Suddenly, the band stops and Hendrix shouts the famous line, "Excuse me, while I kiss the sky." The band comes back in to end the verse as Hendrix plays a short melody reminiscent of the opening solo riff.

0:52 | Verse 2 The music of verse 1 repeats with new lyrics.

1:12 | Bridge and Short Solo A new section of music moves away from the verse as Hendrix yells, "Help me!" The next part needs to be listened to on headphones. I want you to listen to the cool guitar solo Hendrix is playing, but then go back and listen again to all of the strange dialogue taking place in the background. Full of reverb and soft in the overall mix of the song, it's hard to tell what he is saying, but it adds to the dreamlike atmosphere.

1:35 | Introduction Return The solo-style riff from the opening of the song returns, but now the disembodied Hendrix voice that was in the background of the last section acts as added vocal percussion.

1:52 | Verse 3 Same as the first two verses, but there is an added ferocity in the electric guitar sound.

2:15 | Bridge 2 and Effects Solo The bridge returns and leads into a new guitar solo that is laden with effects. Sometimes, the guitar sounds like a bell, or an alarm, other times, like a moan. And all the time, Hendrix says "purple haze" in the background.

YES

Played: **PROGRESSIVE ROCK**

⚡ PLAYLIST ⚡

"Looking Around" (1969)

"Time and a Word" (1970)

"Starship Trooper" (1971)

"I've Seen All Good People" (1971)

"Roundabout" (1971)

"Close to the Edge" (1972)

"Wonderous Stories" (1977)

"Tempus Fugit" (1980)

"Owner of a Lonely Heart" (1983)

"Final Eyes" (1987)

"The Calling" (1996)

"In the Presence Of" (2001)

"Fly from Here" (2011)

Yes recording Fragile *at Advision Studios in London, 1971*

The original lineup of Yes, 1969 (l to r: Tony Kaye, Bill Bruford, Jon Anderson (back), Chris Squire (front), and Peter Banks)

The band Yes is one of the longest-running and most influential groups in what came to be called the progressive rock style. The band has changed its lineup many times over the years but has always featured Chris Squire's signature melodic bass sound at its core. For most of the band's history, the lead singer was Jon Anderson, and his unique alto-tenor singing voice (a very high range) mixed with his mystical lyrics and superb sense of melody helped to define their sound. Although they were popular in the 1970s with songs like "Roundabout," they reached a new level of stardom in the 1980s with their song "Owner of a Lonely Heart" (written by new guitarist Trevor Rabin). This opened the door for the resurgence of many progressive rock bands of the '70s, including the Moody Blues and Genesis.

HISTORICAL FACT/SOCIAL CONNECTIONS

Coming out of psychedelic rock at the end of the 1960s, the idea of progressive rock was to bring in even more musical influences to rock and roll. Yes frequently used formal structures from European classical music (such as the suite), featured virtuosic playing, recorded concept albums, and used expanded instrumentation, particularly the use of new keyboard instruments. They also created a unique vocal sound by combining the techniques they had learned in British boys' choirs, and the sounds of rock harmony singing from groups like the Beach Boys, the Beatles, and the Byrds.

SONG FACTS: "STARSHIP TROOPER" (1971)

Written by Jon Anderson, Chris Squire, and Steve Howe
Released on Atlantic Records, February 1971

"Starship Trooper" comes from the band's third album, but it was the first record to feature guitarist Steve Howe (replacing Peter Banks). Howe's accomplished playing was an inspiration to the other band members, and the result was a record that pushed the boundaries of the progressive rock sound. Also on the album are Jon Anderson (vocals), Chris Squire (bass), Tony Kaye (keyboards), and Bill Bruford (drums). The title of the song comes from a science fiction novel by Robert Heinlein, but the lyrics have little to do with the book. The lyrics defy literal interpretation and instead use Anderson's interests in mysticism, nature, and outer space travel to create an image of an interconnected universe. The starship trooper has traveled the universe, but the singer still finds truth in family and his knowledge of the land.

TRY THIS AT HOME

The author, (left), interviews the band at the Rock and Roll Hall of Fame and Museum, 2013

Construct your own progressive rock master-piece. Start as wild as you want it to be, or it can be a fanciful tale that comments on real world issues. Next, think about the songs on the album and how they will tell your story in multiple parts. Are all the lyrics presented by a narrator, or are there individual characters telling each story? Is it a mix of voices? What kinds of instrumentation will you use for the music? Last, but not least, it's time to make your own gatefold album cover. Look at some of the covers by Yes cover artist Roger Dean for inspiration, but don't feel locked into a single style. Part of the idea of progressive rock is pushing the boundaries, so get creative.

LISTENING GUIDE

"STARSHIP TROOPER"

This song features three distinct sections and each of them is given a different name on the album cover. This makes the song a suite. The three parts are I. Life Seeker, II. Disillusion, and III. Würm. The guide below represents the major structural ideas of each section.

0:00 | Life Seeker It begins with a powerful series of notes that come back over and over again during the next 3 minutes.

In fact, listen to how the band evolves the entire form of this section by moving the music through a number of small ideas: the opening notes, the vocal melody (0:15), mellow vibes (0:36), and a bridge (1:51). Each of these ideas is used several times to create the whole section. See if you can hear each time one of them returns. A favorite little bit of mine is the great bass melody played by Squire at 1:41.

3:16 | Disillusion This section is made up of three new musical ideas. The first part opens with Steve Howe's extraordinary acoustic guitar picking. Over this Anderson, Squire, and Howe harmonize to a beautiful melody.

The second part features a vocal buildup on long-held notes as the bass and guitar pick out various countermelodies. I really love listening to all the voices overlapping in this part.

The last part of Disillusion is more traditional as we get a verselike melody sung over the music of the band. Think about Anderson's voice for a moment. How is it different from many of the other rock music voices we have listened to so far?

5:36 | The Würm The name of this section comes from a winding river in Germany, and I always envision this musical journey at the end of the suite as a trip down the river.

This entire part is based on a descending three-note pattern that starts on D, moves down to B flat, and then ends on a low G. All the music you hear comes from the band members jamming around those three notes. It's quite easy to grab your favorite instrument and jam along with the music—or even play it without the recording having everyone in your family play a part.

The music slowly fades out—as if it could actually go on forever.

PINK FLOYD

Played: **SPACE ROCK/PROGRESSIVE ROCK/ROCK**

⌁ PLAYLIST ⌁

"Arnold Layne" (1967)

"Interstellar Overdrive" (1967)

"A Saucerful of Secrets" (1968)

"Atom Heart Mother" (1970)

"Echoes" (1971)

"Time" (1973)

"Shine on You Crazy Diamond" (1975)

"Another Brick in the Wall, Part 2" (1979)

"Learning to Fly" (1987)

"Keep Talking" (1994)

TRY THIS AT HOME

Even though you don't have a time machine to take your family back to 1966 to enjoy the psychedelic scene at the UFO Club in London, you can build your own rock club in your house! Your light show can be a bunch of flashlights with colored gels put over them. Use a computer screensaver as a psychedelic laser show. Try making your own liquid light show based on the classic ones from the '60s—there are plenty of places on the Internet that explain how to do it safely. What will you wear? How about food to serve? There are a lot of fun ways to create your own musical club scene. Make it a party and invite the neighbors!

Pink Floyd in 1972 (l to r: Nick Mason, David Gilmour, Roger Waters, and Richard Wright)

In the late 1960s, the band Pink Floyd was often called space rock, due to the science fiction themes present in their lyrics and their reliance on new recording technologies and synthesizers to make "outer-space" sounds. Pink Floyd began in 1965 and originally consisted of four members: Roger Waters (bass), Richard "Rick" Wright (keyboards), Nick Mason (percussion), and Syd Barrett (guitar and vocals). When Pink Floyd went into the studio to record their second album in 1968, it was clear that Syd Barrett, who had been behaving very strangely on tour for the first album, was becoming mentally ill. The band eventually decided to replace him with Barrett's old friend David Gilmour, an accomplished musician whose technical ability as a guitarist pushed the band to a new musical level and tightened up their often-sporadic playing. The music of Pink Floyd can take you on a fantastic sonic journey and is best listened to while relaxing in a dimly lit room, or one with a full-on laser light show (which many people, including myself, have done over the years).

HISTORICAL FACT/SOCIAL CONNECTIONS

In 1966, London's underground club scene was growing and promoters were looking for musical groups that could help create the type of "happenings" that were occurring in the East Village of New York and the Haight-Ashbury section of San Francisco. At the same time, many young space rock musicians saw their own musical experimentations as a mixture of San Francisco–based psychedelic rock and British progressive rock. In 1966, Pink Floyd began performing at places like the UFO Club in London, where they soon became the house band. The UFO Club was run and owned by their management team of Peter Jenner and Andrew King, who pushed the band to think about their shows as spectacle. This lesson stayed with them for the rest of their career and led to several famous stage shows including the one for their 1979 album *The Wall*.

ink Floyd in 1967 with Syd Barrett

Vritten by Richard Wright, Roger Vaters, and David Gilmour

eleased on Columbia Records, eptember 1975

his song is the lion's share of the 1975 oncept album *Wish You Were Here* bout Syd Barrett, the original singer and ader of Pink Floyd. Rock legend has it at Barrett even wandered in to Abbey oad Studios to visit while the band as recording. While the album tried to eal with the fact that their talented and reative friend had become ill, and the ct that the band needed to move on thout him, it also looked at their current osition within the music industry. Waters as beginning to notice that they now ad to produce new music under the essure of deadlines and perform live all e time. This was no longer something ey were doing just for fun. *Wish You ere Here* dealt with themes of insanity, enation, and artistic challenges—all ings Waters would return to again on e Wall.

LISTENING GUIDE

"SHINE ON YOU CRAZY DIAMOND"

It is with this recording that we reach the apex of the multipart rock song in this book. "Shine on You Crazy Diamond" is a nine-part suite that was actually split into two sections on the album. The album opens with section one (containing parts I–IV) and the second side of the record ends with section two (parts VI–IX). In total the suite is more than 25 minutes of music. So I have given you the basic outline and the timings are based on the two separate sections. Sit back, enjoy, and use your imagination.

0:00 | Part 1: Introduction The long drone sounds of synthesizers dominate the opening. At 2:08, an electric guitar enters playing a slow, lonesome blues solo.

3:54 | Part II: Four-Note Theme This section begins with a four-note melodic shape played on the guitar: B flat, up to F, down to G, and then back up to E. This serves as a theme for this section and returns over and over again. There is a second guitar solo by Gilmour that slowly builds to a climax.

6:29 | Part III: Another Solo The guitar solo of Part II fades into a synthesizer solo. We then get Gilmour's third guitar solo!

8:41 | Part IV: Shine On This is the first part to feature lyrics sung by Waters supported by female backing vocals. There are several verse sections separated by guitar melodies. Listen for the Hammond B3 played by Wright.

11:09 | Part IV: Shine on You Crazy Saxophone The first half of the song ends with a saxophone solo by Gilmour's friend, musician Dick Parry. It starts out mellow and builds up to the end as it fades out on some improvisational runs. On the actual album, this leads into the song "Welcome to the Machine," but here we will continue with the second section of "Shine on You Crazy Diamond" (Parts VI–IX).

Section Two

0:00 | Part V: Winds of Change This part opens the second half with synthesizer sounds and a guitar solo much like part I opened the first half. But you will notice things are much more active in this section. The solos are more aggressive and the drums played by Mason feature much more swing.

4:39 | Part VI: Shine on Redux This section opens with the electric guitar playing the melody sung by Waters from back in part IV. The vocals reenter and add to the Shine on story.

6:09 | Part VII: Jazzy Diamonds In this section, Mason and Wright really get to "shine" playing a funk-inspired groove. Wright plays a Clavinet and a Minimoog, and Gilmour adds his best funky guitar licks.

9:07 | Part IX: Goodbye to Syd The entire 25 minutes ends with a sad and slow melody played on the synthesizer, accompanied by piano chords.

Played: **HARD ROCK/HEAVY METAL**

⚡ PLAYLIST ⚡

"Black Sabbath" (1970)

"War Pigs" (1970)

"Paranoid" (1970)

"Iron Man" (1970)

"Supernaut" (1972)

"Symptom of the Universe" (1975)

"Neon Knights" (1980)

"The Mob Rules" (1982)

"I" (1992)

"End of the Beginning" (2013)

TRY THIS AT HOME

Use the idea of the band Black Sabbath and the lyrics of "War Pigs" to think about the historical period of the late 1960s and early 1970s. Think about what was happening in the world and how the music of Black Sabbath responded to it. Have each family member research an important historical event from the time period. How does the world they describe in the song compare to the world around you now?

If you were going to form your own heavy metal band, what would you talk about in your lyrics? And have some fun with it: What's the name of your band? Does the group have a logo?

The band Black Sabbath was formed in Birmingham, England, in 1968 by four working class kids: Geezer Butler (bass), Tony Iommi (guitar), Bill Ward (drums), Ozzy Osbourne (vocals). They originally wanted to be a blues-based hard rock band (similar to Led Zeppelin) but eventually changed their sound, dropping many of the blues elements and focusing on the idea of the guitar riff and dark-themed lyrics. This new sound would soon come to be called heavy metal, and for this reason, many people consider Black Sabbath to be the first metal band. (If you want evidence, just listen to the song "Iron Man," it's all riffs and lyrical disaster). The band saw many personnel changes over the years, and included musicians such as vocalist Ronnie James Dio (who invented the "rock horns"—really, he did), drummer Vinny Appice, and keyboard player Geoff Nicholls.

HISTORICAL FACT/SOCIAL CONNECTIONS

Soldiers in Vietnam

So let's get something out of the way right from the start: The look, sound, and lyrical themes of Black Sabbath deal with doom, destruction, witches, demons, the occult, and other such evil stuff. But what many people misinterpret is that the band was not endorsing or promoting these things. In fact, they got quite good at using these dark images as a way to talk about the world around them. (See the listening guide for "War Pigs") In 1970, the Vietnam War was still going on (with

soldiers dying and no end in site), the antiwar movement continued (and the tragic shootings at Kent State in Ohio made the issue even more pressing), and the peace and love vibe of psychedelic rock and hippie movement was waning. The sound of Black Sabbath was a response to this bleak period.

SONG FACTS: "WAR PIGS" (1970)

Ozzy Osbourne

Written by Iommi, Osbourne, Butler, and Ward

Released on Vertigo Records, September 1970

This song was written by the four band members and is the first song on their 1970 album *Paranoid*. Initially, it was a fantasy piece with images of witches, fire, and a Sabbath. Geezer Butler soon rewrote the lyrics to take an antiwar stance, using the images of witches, wizards, and demons as an analogy for the war mongers and politicians in contemporary society. Butler claims that he had the issues of the Vietnam War in his mind (although Ozzy claims he did not). Either way, the song can now be heard as a powerful and fighting vision of what the band members felt about the conflicts of the late 1960s.

The version of this song that appears on the *Paranoid* album contains an extended coda called "Luke's Wall." The two sections, together, add up to 7 minutes and 55 seconds.

"WAR PIGS/LUKE'S WALL"

LISTENING GUIDE

0:00 | Introduction The electric guitar, bass, and drums start the song. Notice the distortion of the electric guitar (it sounds fuzzy, like it's breaking up and overdriven—a hallmark of heavy metal).

0:52 | Verse 1 The verse starts with the ticking of the high-hat cymbals interrupted with blasts of sound from the guitar, bass, and drums. What does this make you think of? Ozzy's voice enters singing the lyrics. He is technically not a great singer—his voice often wavers when he holds out high notes, or his musical pitch is off by just a little bit; but listen to how much character his voice has and how he draws you into the story. This makes him a great rock singer.

1:46 | Instrumental Break The instruments all begin playing the main riff of the song and begin to build up the activity.

2:07 | Verse 2 Ozzy sings a similar melody to the first verse—but listen to how the instruments differ at this time. The riff from the instrumental break has now energized the entire song.

3:10 | Instrumental Break 2

3:30 | Guitar Solo The basic drums and bass groove of the instrumental break continues and Tony Iommi plays a guitar solo above it. Listen to the way that Iommi bends the notes by pushing on the strings while he is playing. He plays groups of notes in quick succession and then holds out a single note in contrast. Even though the solo showcases his technique, it never loses the melody.

4:30 | Verse 3 After the solo, the energy of the song dissipates and we return to the quiet high-hat ticking and instrumental interruptions of the first verse. This is a good way to build up again for the second part of the song.

5:44 | Guitar Solo 2, "Luke's Wall" Musically, this second guitar solo fits in nicely with the end of the main song, and even sounds pretty similar, but as it goes along it begins to move farther and farther away from the main riff of "War Pigs."

CREAM

Played: **BLUES REVIVAL/HARD ROCK**

PLAYLIST

"I Feel Free" (1966)

"Spoonful" (1966)

"I'm So Glad" (1966)

"Strange Brew" (1967)

"Sunshine of Your Love" (1967)

"Tales of Brave Ulysses" (1967)

"White Room" (1968)

"Born Under a Bad Sign" (1968)

"Crossroads" (1968)

"Badge" (1969)

Cream was labeled as a supergroup from the moment they started, meaning that all the musicians were famous before they formed the band. It also means that there was an attempt to market the music (to some extent) on that fame (and of course this still happens frequently today in popular music). Ginger Baker (drums), Eric Clapton (guitar, vocals), and Jack Bruce (vocals, bass) were considered some of the top players in England's blues revival scene when they formed in 1966, and because of that, they decided to call the group Cream (as in "cream of the crop").

Eric Clapton, 1967

HISTORICAL FACT/SOCIAL CONNECTIONS

In the 1960s many British musicians fell in love with the sound of American blues music, especially the sounds of Chess Records artists. Early recordings of the blues became popular in England as American soldiers brought records over during World War II, and the port cities of London and Liverpool also helped to keep the trade of music flowing after the war. Muddy Waters made a big impact in England when he toured there in 1958. Several British musicians, including Cyril Davies and Alexis Korner, began playing in a style that tried to match the sound of those early blues records as accurately as possible. Eventually, there was an entire scene that included the Rolling Stones, Blues Incorporated, John Mayall and the Bluesbreakers, and the Yardbirds. The Yardbirds are particularly worthy of note, because three stellar guitarists played with them during the '60s: Eric Clapton (1963–1965), Jeff Beck (1965–1966), and Jimmy Page (1966–1968).

SONG FACTS: "SUNSHINE OF YOUR LOVE" (1967)

Cream live at the Whisky A Go Go in 1967

Written by Jack Bruce, Pete Brown, Eric Clapton

Released on Atco Records, November 1967

The music of Cream is steeped in the traditions of delta and electric blues. Many of the songs on their first album, *Fresh Cream,* are covers of songs by artists like Willie Dixon, Robert Johnson, and Skip James. But, like many of the bands we've discussed in this chapter, they started to mix it up with elements from psychedelic rock to create a new blues sound for the 1960s. "Sunshine of Your Love" is from their second album *Disraeli Gears,* and it is the perfect example of that blend. To see a cool visual that presents the concept of a psychedelic blues, check out the album cover.

TRY THIS AT HOME

Learn to play guitar. Really, just do it! Many great players like Clapton started by just sitting in their rooms listening to records and trying to copy the sounds that they heard. You can try it several different ways. Just sit and listen, and then try to copy what you hear. In this method, you don't need to worry about proper technique or form, just play until it sounds good. The second way is to take some actual lessons. Look around your community. Often, there are great local music teachers willing to offer lessons, and sometimes you can even find a beginner class for groups that teaches all ages. There is no better way to inspire your kids than learning right alongside them. The last way is made possible by the great world of the Internet! There are so many options online, such as YouTube videos, paid websites, Skype teachers, and even video games like Rocksmith that use a real guitar and not a plastic game controller.

LISTENING GUIDE

"SUNSHINE OF YOUR LOVE"

The music here is all about a powerful bass and guitar riff that runs throughout almost the entire song. There is something about the way that the notes bend and slide in the repeated riff that sounds very much like Hendrix. Clapton gets his guitar sound in the song by using some distortion and a wah-wah pedal that makes the sound literally go wah-wah-wah-wah as the guitarist steps on and off the pedal.

0:00 | Instrumental Introduction The song opens with the foundational bass and guitar riff. The drums enter with an interesting rhythm. Instead of playing with the accent on the backbeat that is so common to rock and roll, Ginger Baker reverses it and plays with the main accent on beats 1 and 3 of the 4/4 measures. The format of the band is called a power trio, consisting of just three instruments: drums, bass, and guitar. Listen to how all the music comes from just that basic arrangement.

0:17 | Verse 1 A great first line sets the mood for the entire song. I love the imagery presented by the words "when lights close their tired eyes." I always think of how the artificial light of streetlights and lamps is being replaced by the powerful emotional light of the person he loves. Notice that the only drums playing are the bass, snare, and tom-toms. There are no cymbals in the verse.

0:50 | Chorus The chorus is easy to identify since the main riff of the song ends. Now the guitar and bass play a halting rhythm. But the rising vocals and the added power in the drums keeps things moving and gives us a feeling that things are continuously building up—like a sunrise. Notice that Baker adds the cymbals into his rhythm to give the chorus a bigger sound.

1:06 | Verse 2 Listen to the lyrics. He is describing the transformational moment of finally being with the one you love. There are a lot of ways to interpret this section, so discuss the lyrics as is appropriate for the age level at home.

1:44 | Chorus 2

2:00 | Guitar Solo The solo actually plays though a full verse/chorus cycle of the music and features a great mix of blues and psychedelic rock.

2:50 | Verse 3 This verse starts with the reestablishment of the riff (much like the instrumental introduction).

3:33 | Chorus 3

The Staple Singers, 1975

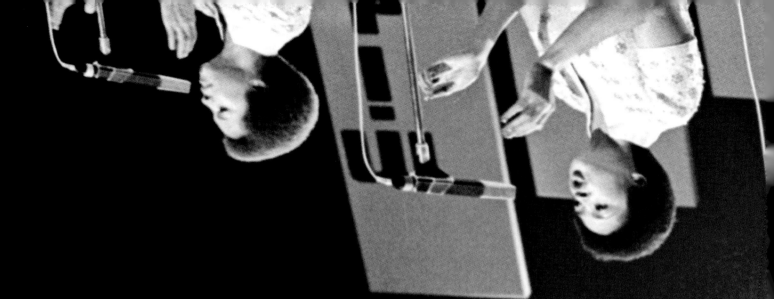

CHAPTER 3:
⚡ DEEP SOUL ⚡

– PLAYLIST –

"Mess Around" (1953)

"I Got a Woman" (1955)

"Hallelujah I Love Her So" (1956)

"What'd I Say—Parts I & II" (1959)

"Night Time Is the Right Time" (1959)

"Georgia on My Mind" (1960)

"Hit the Road Jack" (1961)

"I Can't Stop Loving You" (1962)

"Eleanor Rigby" (1968)

"America the Beautiful" (1976)

"Baby Grand" (with Billy Joel) (1986)

Ray Charles in the studio, 1962

If we are going to talk about soul music, the story has to start with the amazing piano player, singer, songwriter, arranger, bandleader, and businessman, Ray Charles (1930–2004). He was born in Albany, Georgia, and began to lose his sight when he was very young. As a result, he attended the St. Augustine School for the Deaf and the Blind in Florida. By the age of fifteen, he was playing with bands in the local area, and in 1950 he made his first professional recordings with producer Henry Stone. His big break came in 1952 when he signed a recording contract with Atlantic Records, leading to a string of R&B hits during the late 1950s. Charles was eventually nicknamed the "Genius of Soul," and even though I don't like to throw the term *genius* around much, in this case, it is deserved.

HISTORICAL FACT/SOCIAL CONNECTIONS

Charles's mid-50s music recorded at Atlantic consisted of rocking rhythm and blues tunes like "Mess Around," a great example of his upbeat boogie-woogie piano style, influenced by musicians like Fats Domino. By 1955, Charles started to mix that R&B sound with gospel music, which led to the development of the soul music sound. It's important to remember that rock and roll comes from a mixture of American music styles, so what Charles was doing was not entirely new. But his mixture of gospel and R&B happened in ways that made some people uncomfortable. Charles took a number of gospel songs and changed the lyrics from a sacred text (in praise of God) to a secular text (of the material world). In this process, the hymn "It Must Be Jesus," originally by the Southern Tones, became "I Got a Woman." The traditional tune "This Little Light of Mine"

...amously recorded by the Clara Ward Singers) became "This Little Girl of Mine." It's not hard to imagine how these changes upset the gospel community, who saw Charles's new versions as sacrilegious. How could you take a song that was in praise of the Lord and change it to ...e about a relationship with a girl?

"HALLELUJAH I LOVE HER SO"

The entire song is only 2 minutes and 36 seconds, so if you're reading this book in order, this will seem like a shock after some of the half-hour epics in chapter 2.

0:00 | Instrumental Introduction The song opens with a mid-tempo solo piano played by Charles. The melody and chord progression have overtones of a gospel tune, but when the horns and drums enter, it pulls it immediately closer to rhythm and blues.

0:15 | Verse 1 The lyrics begin to extol the virtues of Charles's girlfriend. Listen to how the band begins to play in what is called stop-time at the 20-second mark. The band stops playing and hits a chord—"bomp"—only in between each phrase of the vocal.

0:33 | Verse 2

0:52 | Bridge The bridge keeps basically the same chord progression, but it is distinguished by the extended use of stop-time, and the way the band quickly runs through a series of hits in each break. Check out the cool word painting as the drummer creates the "knock, knock" sound when Charles sings about his girl knocking at the door.

1:05 | Verse 3

1:25 | Saxophone Solo The solo is performed by tenor saxophone player Donald Wilkerson. Can you hear how it uses a variation of the melody that Charles is singing in the verses?

1:45 | Verse 4

1:58 | Verse 5

2:16 | Ending Vamp

SONG FACTS: "HALLELUJAH I LOVE HER SO" (1956)

Written by Ray Charles

Released as a single on Atlantic Records, 1956

Some of Charles's songs were altered versions of actual gospel spirituals, but this one was more likely inspired by the sound of Dorothy Love Coates and her group the Gospel Harmonettes. Even so, you can hear what might have been a gospel tune in the title of the song, hallelujah I love Him so, referring to God—but Charles replaces the Him at the center of the song with a woman (her). The analogy to the spiritual world works great here. Charles sings "Hallelujah!" (praise Him), as he professes his love for the unnamed woman. It takes his emotions and the power of love and pushes it into the realm of a spiritual experience while the music thumps and grooves with a rhythm and blues swing.

Ray Charles

DESTINATIONS

While Charles developed as a performer and songwriter, he also paid close attention to the business of the music industry. In 1961, he even opened his own studio and offices called RPM International in Los Angeles. That building at 2107 W. Washington Boulevard is now the home of the Ray Charles Memorial Library, where you can see several small exhibits about Charles's life.

SOLOMON BURKE

Played: **RHYTHM AND BLUES/COUNTRY/"ROCK AND SOUL"**

⌁ PLAYLIST ⌁

"Presents for Christmas" (1955)

"This Little Ring" (1960)

"Just Out of Reach (of My Two Open Arms)" (1961)

"Cry to Me" (1962)

"Home in Your Heart" (1963)

"If You Need Me" (1963)

"He'll Have to Go" (1964)

"Everybody Needs Somebody to Love" (1964)

"Got to Get You Off My Mind" (1965)

"I Can't Stop" (1969)

"Sidewalks, Fences and Walls" (1979)

"None of Us Are Free" (2002)

"Up to the Mountain" (with Patty Griffin) (2006)

Solomon Burke press photo, 1965

Solomon Burke (1940–2010) was born and raised in Philadelphia. From a very early age, he was active as a Christian preacher in his church, The House of God for All People. His spiritual beliefs and his love of music led him to form a gospel group during his teens. After some local success as a singer, Burke made his way to New York and quickly signed a recording contract with Atlantic Records. Ray Charles may have created the blueprint for soul music during his time at the label in the late 1950s, but it was Burke who took it to the next level and helped to shape the sound of soul in the 1960s. He soon gave himself the nickname the "King of Rock and Soul," which stuck with him the rest of his life and even led to his famous stage routine of wearing a crown and a cape and sitting on the stage in a throne.

Burke in the studio with Jerry Wexler, 1960

HISTORICAL FACT/SOCIAL CONNECTIONS

Atlantic Records was created in New York City in 1944 by Ahmet Ertegun and Herb Abramson. Along with producer Jerry Wexler and recording engineer Tom Dowd, they helped to make some of the greatest rock and roll music of all time. When Burke made his way to New York in 1960, it was with the idea of selling a song he wrote called "This Little Ring," to Atlantic Records. He met with Ahmet Ertegun and Jerry Wexler in their office and within moments he was signed to the label. They soon informed Burke that Ray Charles had just left Atlantic for another record label and they needed a new singer to take his place. A funny footnote to the story—Burke once told me that they never even listened to the recording he brought with him to the office that day. They signed him on his reputation alone!

Burke performing live, 1965

Written by Jerry Wexler, Bert Berns,
Solomon Burke

Released on Atlantic Records,
February 1964

This is one of those songs that many people don't recognize from the name, but once the music starts playing, they remember it right away. As it turns out, many people have heard it in one of the various cover versions made over the years by groups like the Rolling Stones and the Blues Brothers (who perform it as one of the final numbers in their 1980 movie *The Blues Brothers*). You will notice that the music of this song is fairly static, like the music of James Brown discussed in chapter 1. There are not a lot of complicated chord changes or multiple sections. This song is all about the rhythm, the feel, and the message that Burke is singing and preaching. As Burke says just before the first verse begins, "if everybody sings this song we can save the whole world."

"EVERYBODY NEEDS SOMEBODY TO LOVE"

0:00 | Instrumental Introduction I just love the opening of this song. It starts so simply, but gets you in the groove and the mood right away. The sax blows, "boo-doomp," and then the guitar and bass follow up with a series of strummed eighth notes that sound like they are singing "do-doo-do-doo-do-do-do-dooo." At the end of every other count of four the guitarist slides his finger down the neck of the guitar, making a "boowwwwww" sound. But listen really closely. Can you hear what's going on in the background, behind the music? There are people talking to each other, clapping, moving around, as if the whole thing were happening in a real concert—or maybe even in a church.

0:08 | Spoken Section Burke's background as preacher comes to the forefront here. He preaches the sermon. Once he starts talking, all the people in the background start to pay attention to him and participate in the classic gospel call and response. Burke once told me that the music was taken straight from a musical vamp he performed at his church (and is fairly common in many African American churches in the United States). It's important to realize that this section is a full one-third of the song. Burke did not hear it as simply a setup. This is a major part of the song.

1:00 | Verse 1 The song finally moves into the verse. Burke sings the main melody, but if you are really paying attention, you will hear that the band doesn't change what it is doing. Listen to his voice. You can hear the emotion and inflections of each word and phrase. The recording even distorts at several points when his big powerful voice pushes the recording equipment to its limits.

1:32 | Chorus The music is still the same, but now Burke sings the hook, "I need you, you, you." The backing vocals join in singing along with him and adding rhythmic handclaps.

1:47 | Bridge This is the first time the music changes. The backing vocals sing out with "ohhs," the bass plays a new bouncing melody, and the horns get in on the action.

2:00 | Chorus 2 The music jumps back into the main groove, but now the trumpet and the rest of the horn section takes part in the call and response. Burke begins to talk to the audience again, asking for a witness (a common call made by a preacher to the church). It just builds and builds, and jams to the end with a final fadeout. We get the feeling that this could go on for another hour.

ARETHA FRANKLIN

Played: **SOUL**

⟶ PLAYLIST ⟵

"Soulsville" (1964)

"I Never Loved a Man (The Way I Love You)" (1967)

"Respect" (1967)

"(You Make Me Feel Like) A Natural Woman" (1967)

"Chain of Fools" (1967)

"Think" (1968)

"I Say a Little Prayer" (1968)

"Spirit in the Dark" (1970)

"Rock Steady" (1972)

"Day Dreaming" (1972)

"Sisters Are Doin' It for Themselves" (with the Eurythmics) (1985)

"A Rose Is Still a Rose" (1998)

"Wonderful" (2003)

Aretha Franklin, 1967

Aretha Franklin was born in Memphis, Tennessee, in 1942, but soon moved to the city she has called home for most of her life, Detroit. Her father, C. L. Franklin, was a famous preacher at the New Bethel Baptist Church, and young Aretha frequently performed as part of the church gospel choir. By the age of ten she was meeting and learning from some of the world's greatest gospel singers who came to perform at her father's church, including Mahalia Jackson, Clara Ward, and Sam Cooke. She recorded her first gospel record at the age of fifteen, and when she turned eighteen she signed to Columbia Records and recorded a number of great songs like "Soulsville." She really hit her stride when she began working with Atlantic Records in 1967. Jerry Wexler encouraged her to bring out the gospel power in her voice, and within a very short period of time, she earned the nickname "the Queen of Soul."

Aretha Franklin live in Cleveland, 1983

HISTORICAL FACT/SOCIAL CONNECTIONS

Soul music may have come from a mixture of black church music and rhythm and blues, but it also incorporated other ideas. The music was presented as having "soul," which of course has a spiritual meaning, but also taps into a musical sense of having emotion, as in having a "soulful" melody. But by the 1960s, the term also began to represent the struggles of African Americans in the segregated United States. Soul was code for blackness. It represented an attitude that said that each and every person was someone important, and it projected a sense of confidence. As James Brown sang, "I've got soul and I'm superbad." As such, soul music quickly became the soundtrack of the civil rights movement, which had already adopted many old spirituals as rallying songs during marches and protests.

SONG FACTS: "RESPECT" (1965)

Written by Otis Redding
Released on Atlantic Records,
August 1967

This song was originally written and recorded by Stax Records recording artist Otis Redding in 1965. His version of the song is a bit of macho bragging, asking a woman for respect in his house when he comes home from work. So why did Aretha choose to record it? She flips the respect of asking for... ar man for everything she does in the house for their family. This was a bold statement to make in 1967 in an era that saw the rise of the women's liberation movement. Aretha was not only singing these words as a woman—but as a black woman. Suddenly, the soulful macho song as originally written by Redding was transformed into a statement of black pride/women's rights for a generation.

...nd it was still fun to dance to and sing along with!

TRY THIS AT HOME

Talk with your family about issues of equality in the 1960s. Think about issues about gender, race, and class. How were people treated differently and what kinds of changes did various groups of people fight for to make a change? Now think about how things are different today. Have things improved? How are some things still the same? Are there particular groups of people fighting for equality around the world now? Are there songs that talk about these issues today? Hint: Think about Lady Gaga's "Born This Way" (2011).

"RESPECT"

LISTENING GUIDE

0:00 | Introduction This song sounds so simple on the surface, but that's because all the various pieces fit together so well. Listen closely to this introduction and you will hear drums, bass, guitar, piano, organ, and a full horn section of saxophones. And each instrument is doing something interesting. Listen to the song a number of times and focus your attention on just one instrument for the whole song. Start with the bass. You might be amazed to hear all the great melodic rhythms it plays.

0:10 | Verse 1 The backing vocals enter with a "woo," to kick the song into the first verse. Aretha's voice attacks the first line with a lot of energy, "What, you want." Listen to how she strings all the short little phrases together to make the whole verse feel connected. At the end of the section, Aretha sings the refrain "All I'm asking for is a little respect," and the background singers enter into a call and response with her as they sing, "Just a little bit."

0:30 | Verse 2

0:51 | Verse 3 Listen to how the piano really pounds out the chords here giving it a strong presence in the overall mix.

1:12 | Saxophone Solo The horn section plays long, held-out chords while the tenor saxophone takes a solo.

1:28 | Verse 4 Aretha holds-out the first word of the first phrase in the verse, "Ohhhhhhh, your kisses." When I hear her do that I am always struck by how much that sounds like the long held notes of the saxophones in the last section. It makes for a great musical transition back into the verse, and it also makes sense lyrically as she swoons over her man's kisses. This verse is one of the first times you can really hear the organ clearly on its own, so listen closely.

1:50 | Stop-Time, Spell It Out Without a doubt the most famous part of the song. The band plays in typical soul music stop-time—only hitting a few chords in between Aretha's vocal phrases. In case you didn't get the point of the song, the Queen of Soul literally spells it out for you, "R – E – S – P – E – C – T!" If you ever wondered what she says at the end it's "Take care . . . TCB" (Taking Care of Business).

1:58 | The Band Rocks It Out to the End The end of the song is the most directly connected to Aretha's gospel upbringing. The band settles into the groove but also kicks up the energy a bit more. Aretha and the backing vocalists begin to ad lib on the lyrics and melody. If you listen to live versions of the song from the late 1960s, sometimes they actually begin to make it sound more and more like a soul-inspired gospel jam.

WILSON PICKETT

Played: **RHYTHM AND BLUES/SOUL**

⟍ PLAYLIST ⟍

"In the Midnight Hour" (1965)

"634-5789 (Soulsville U.S.A.)" (1966)

"Ninety Nine and a Half (Won't Do)" (1966)

"Land of 1,000 Dances" (1966)

"Mustang Sally" (1966)

"Soul Dance Number Three" (1967)

"Funky Broadway" (1967)

"I'm In Love" (1967)

"Don't Knock My Love" (1971)

"Funk Factory" (1972)

SONG FACTS: "LAND OF 1,000 DANCES"

Written by Chris Kenner

Released on *The Exciting Wilson Pickett*, **Atlantic Records, May 1966**

This song was recorded at FAME studios in Muscle Shoals, Alabama, and features some of the great studio musicians of the era: Chips Moman, Spooner Oldham, and Roger Hawkins. This studio was famous for creating recordings that sounded like they were happening live, and many other soul singers recorded their including Percy Sledge and Aretha Franklin.

Wilson Pickett performs

Wilson Pickett (1941–2006) is another one of the all-time great rhythm and blues and soul singers. He cowrote many of his own songs and his interpretations of songs originally recorded by other artists have become the definitive version. Pickett was born in Prattville, Alabama and, like many fellow soul singers, he got his start singing gospel music in church. His powerful and gritty voice gave him a forceful presence in his early vocal group, the Falcons (which also included singers Eddie Floyd and Sir Mack Rice). The majority of his solo records were released on Atlantic Records, and he recorded at some of the most famous studios in the American South: Stax, FAME, and American studios.

TRY THIS AT HOME

Dancing the Watusi

One of the great things about this song, and about so many classic soul tunes, is that it is a great piece of music to dance to. Now I know many people don't like to dance. You might be afraid, you might worry that someone will think your doing it wrong. But here's the thing: None of that matters—you can do this in your own living room with no one watching. Kids love to dance and so should you. The cool thing to do for this song is to learn to do all of the dances that are mentioned by Pickett. Welcome to the Internet! You would not believe how many short videos will show you how to do all of these great dance moves (this endeavor, alone, makes for a great activity). But then try to have everyone do the dances themselves. Once you're really confident, (or at least not falling down), you can try to string them together. If you need some inspiration, go look at the dancing during the Ray Charles performance of "Shake Your Tail Feather" in the movie *The Blues Brothers* (1980). It shows a whole street full of people trying a number of dances that Charles calls out.

LISTENING GUIDE

"LAND OF 1,000 DANCES"

0:00 | Introduction Wilson Pickett counts off the band, 1, 2, 3… and they respond with everyone playing a big crashing chord. He then does it again. Pickett counts 1, 2, 3, but the actual time signature of this song is 4/4. If you listen closely, you can hear the drummer play the fourth beat just before the band plays the stacked chord.

0:09 | Verse 2 An opening rhythm sets in and the whole band plays the groove. Listen to Pickett's grunts and groans.

Pickett then begins to sing the lyrics of the verse. The words are a set of instructions telling the audience to follow him in a number of well known dance moves: the pony, the bony-moronie (actually a song by Larry Williams from 1957), the mashed potato, the alligator, and the Watusi.

0:37 | Break This break in the action, where most of the instruments drop out except for the drums, contains the famous sing-along lines "Na, na, na, na naaah."

0:56 | Verse 2 In this shortened verse, the saxophone plays in place of Pickett's vocals.

1:18 | Break 2 Back to the drum break and this time it starts with Pickett talking to us, "You know I feel alright." This really gives the recording the sensation of being a live performance. It ends with a return to the "Na, na" sing-along.

1:42 | Verse 3 The third verse returns to Pickett's vocal melody from the first verse. Some of the dances are repeated and some new ones are mentioned as well (the Jerk).

2:05 | Outro The band keeps playing the main groove of the song, but Pickett begins to improvise and encourage the audience to keep dancing, "ahhhh, do it!" The song quickly fades out.

MARVIN GAYE

Played: **MOTOWN/SOUL**

- PLAYLIST -

"Can I Get a Witness" (1963)

"How Sweet It Is (To Be Loved by You)" (1964)

"It Takes Two" (with Kim Weston) (1966)

"Ain't No Mountain High Enough" (with Tammi Terrell) (1967)

"You're All I Need to Get By" (with Tammi Terrell) (1968)

"I Heard It Through the Grapevine" (1968)

"What's Going On" (1971)

"Trouble Man" (1972)

"Let's Get It On" (1973)

"My Mistake (Was to Love You)" (with Diana Ross) (1974)

"Got to Give It Up" (1977)

"Sexual Healing" (1982)

Marvin Gaye, 1971

Marvin Gaye (1939–1984) grew up in Washington, D.C., the son of a Pentecostal preacher, and, like all the artists in this chapter, he developed a strong connection to gospel music. When he was young, Marvin formed a vocal group called The Marquees. The group had only minimal success, but in a strange twist, the singer Harvey Fuqua hired the members of the Marquees to be the new backup singers in his group the Moonglows. In 1960, Gaye met Motown Records owner Berry Gordy, who convinced him to come to Motown. Gaye's early singles there clearly reference Ray Charles's soul sound, as in "Can I Get a Witness." Over time he developed his own sound—which eventually put him at odds with Gordy, who wanted Gaye to continue to record songs using the Motown "formula."

HISTORICAL FACT/SOCIAL CONNECTIONS

During the late 1960s and early 1970s, public support for the Vietnam War in the United States began to wane. I mentioned previously that bands like Black Sabbath were creating a sound that was musically representative of the troubled times in the world, but the social instability made its way into R&B and soul as well. Marvin Gaye's 1971 album *What's Going On* is a concept album that deals with the problems a Vietnam veteran has to confront once returning home to the United States: drug abuse, poverty, and depression. For many veterans, the world seemed like a different place, one they didn't recognize, and many found themselves confronted with an American public who viewed them as anything but heroes. Many veterans became part of the antiwar movement and began to protest the war openly.

Vietnam veterans protest in the Mall, Washington, D.C.

Photo from the What's Going On *album photo shoot*

Written by Al Cleveland, Renaldo Benson, and Marvin Gaye

Released on Motown Records, January 1971

This song represents Gaye's artistic move away from the team-produced Motown sound (see the Supremes entry in chapter and into a personal space including his interest in jazz. There is an amazing live version of the song that was performed 1973 at the Save the Children concert. When you compare it to the recorded version off of the album, you can hear how Gaye's jazz leanings allowed him to take the same melody and twist and turn small variations of it to great effect.

"WHAT'S GOING ON"

LISTENING GUIDE

The three songwriters all shared personal experiences that eventually gave them the final vision for the song's lyrics. Gaye had talked to his brother Frankie, who served in Vietnam for three years. If you listen to the entire album, you'll hear that the end of the last song, "Inner City Blues (Make Me Wanna Holler)" ends with the band starting to play "What's Going On," looping the whole thing back to the start of the album.

0:00 | Ambient Sound and the Instrumental Introduction The song begins with a number of men talking, and it sounds like they are just off in the distance. They greet each other and use a number of African American slang phrases from the 1960s such as "what's happening," "Yeah, brother, like solid," and "Right on." This helps to identify the space of the record right away. The band begins to play as the saxophone wails a short jazzlike melody. Notice that the voices are still talking in the background.

0:18 | Verse 1 The musicians playing on the record were all part of the Motown house band the Funk Brothers, but Gaye allowed them to stretch out and try interesting things on the song. Listen closely to each instrument, and you will hear a number of subtle variations in what they are playing as the song continues.

0:46 | Verse 2 During this verse, I want you to focus on the sound of Marvin Gaye's voice. First of all let's just recognize how fantastic his voice actually is. Listen to how he moves between controlled soft whispers and loud, held-out notes in the high register. If you listen very closely, you will notice that there are actually two versions of his voice singing the song with a slightly different melody. Gaye recorded it two different ways with the idea that he would pick one in the end. When they went to choose, he realized that both of them worked together—awesome.

1:15 | Bridge Finger snaps accentuate the backbeat. A new melody in the vocal features shorter phrases. The string section enters with a legato melody in the background.

1:28 | Chorus Finally the chorus of the song with call and response from the background singers.

1:38 | Postchorus The music returns to the vibe of the introduction. The musicians start to improvise (just listen to that killer bass line played by James Jamerson). The talking voices seem even louder now—as if more people are starting to join the conversation.

2:07 | Verse 3 As Gaye pleads "Mother, mother" the music swells yet again. Now the strings sound out as a full section with its own musical theme. The saxophone wails its own jazz melody in the background. Gaye's two-verse melodies begin to differ from each other more and more, and the background singers' long held notes rise in volume into the foreground.

2:34 | Bridge The music maintains the lush orchestration.

2:48 | Chorus 2 Gaye's vocal delivery seems more forceful than ever as he is now almost shouting over all the other instruments and voices playing in the song. It's quite remarkable the whole thing doesn't fall apart with that many elements.

2:58 | Postchorus 2 The scat vocals intensify with various vocal deliveries from Gaye and the background singers. The crowd keeps talking and talking into the fade. Notice that this section lasts for almost a minute (and on the album, the music riff slides right into the next song, "What's Happening Brother").

THE STAPLE SINGERS

Played: **GOSPEL/SOUL/SOUTHERN SOUL**

~ PLAYLIST ~

"Let Me Ride" (1959)

"Freedom Highway" (1965)

"Heavy Makes You Happy (Sha-Na-Boom Boom)" (1971)

"Love Is Plentiful" (1971)

"Respect Yourself" (1971)

"I'll Take You There" (1972)

"If You're Ready (Come Go with Me)" (1973)

"Be What You Are" (1973)

"Oh La De Da" (1974)

"City in the Sky" (1974)

The Staple Singers

The Staple Singers began in the late 1940s in Chicago. Roebuck "Pops" Staples formed the singing group with his son Pervis and his three daughters, Cleotha, Yvonne, and Mavis. Their early recordings are all pure gospel. In the 1960s, they began to move toward a pop music sound and eventually found a perfect home making soul music for Stax Records in Memphis, TN, during the 1970s. The family sang together in beautiful harmony. As they reached mainstream success, Mavis Staples became a star due to her formidable and emotive vocals.

The Bar-Kays outside of Stax Records in Memphis, TN

HISTORICAL FACT/SOCIAL CONNECTIONS

The Staple Singers perform live at Wattstax

Many of the Staple Singers' songs became popular messages of black pride in post–civil rights era America. For example, the song "Respect Yourself" can be heard simply as a positive personal affirmation, but it was originally written for the group by Luther Ingram and Sir Mack Rice as a direct statement about the need for African Americans to respect themselves and aggressively pursue the betterment of their position in American society (a message that found multiple outlets in popular culture during the 1970s, even in television sitcoms like *The Jeffersons*).

"I'LL TAKE YOU THERE" (1971)

Written by Al Bell

Released on Stax Records, 1972

Written by Al Bell, who became the owner of Stax Records in 1969, this song is a meditation on going to a better place — is it heaven? For Bell this was a very personal meditation. He wrote the song at his father's house after attending the funeral of his younger brother. The song's message of moving to a better place also connected nicely to the message of upward mobility for African Americans in the 1970s. The singer, Mavis Staples, encourages us to come along with her. This also reflects the true meaning of gospel, to spread the good word of God. But that doesn't stop the music from being super funky and soulful.

The original location of the Stax Records studio and offices at 926 E. McLemore venue in Memphis is now an amazing museum dedicated to the history of American soul music. The exhibits talk about the history of the record label, but they also place it into the broader story of soul music discussed in this chapter. If you really want to create a historically conscious trip for your family, then be sure to check out the National Civil Rights Museum a few blocks away in the old Lorraine Hotel — where Dr. Martin Luther King Jr. was assassinated, and where many of the Stax house band members and artists (a racially integrated group) would often go to relax and write songs.

"I'LL TAKE YOU THERE"

LISTENING GUIDE

For this song, I want you to try to pay attention to something for the whole song. Listen to the "space" in the sound of the song. What do I mean by that? Stax Records was famous for recording music so that it felt like it happened in an actual space and not in a barren, clinical studio. For example, just try singing in your own voice something simple (like "Twinkle, Twinkle Little Star") in two or three different rooms in your house — let's say the bedroom, the bathroom, and the living room. If you listen to yourself, you should notice that the space changes the sound of your voice by adding reverb, echo, or even dampening the sound. Now listen for that in this song. You'll hear it right away in the snare drum and bass guitar hit that opens the song.

0:00 | Instrumental Introduction The song opens with the various instruments playing short little ideas and activating the music space. Mavis moans and groans, getting us ready for the song.

0:14 | Vocals Enter The full band enters playing a basic groove that is influenced by Jamaican reggae music. Listen to how the snare drum, the bass guitar, and the guitar "scratches" all play off of each other rhythmically. The music of the song, as a whole, is very static. The entire song is about the interactions of the various instruments and the call and response vocal between Mavis and the rest of her family.

This song is in the key of C and it contains only two chords, C and F. It never changes from that, so this is another great song to have your family play along with.

The song does not have a musical form in the manner we have talked about so far. What it does is ebb and flow with different instruments or groups of instruments moving to the foreground or receding into the background.

Listen carefully to see which ones you can hear. Here are some of the big ones:

1:16 | Electric Piano Featured

1:34 | Electric Guitar Featured

1:44 | Harmonica Featured

1:54 | Bass Guitar Featured with Wurlitzer Piano in Background I love how Mavis imitates the bass line with her voice in this section.

2:10 | Return of Main Vocals talking and talking into the fade. Notice that this section lasts for almost a minute (and on the album, the music riff slides right into the next song, "What's Happening Brother").

Paul Simonon of the Clash, 1979

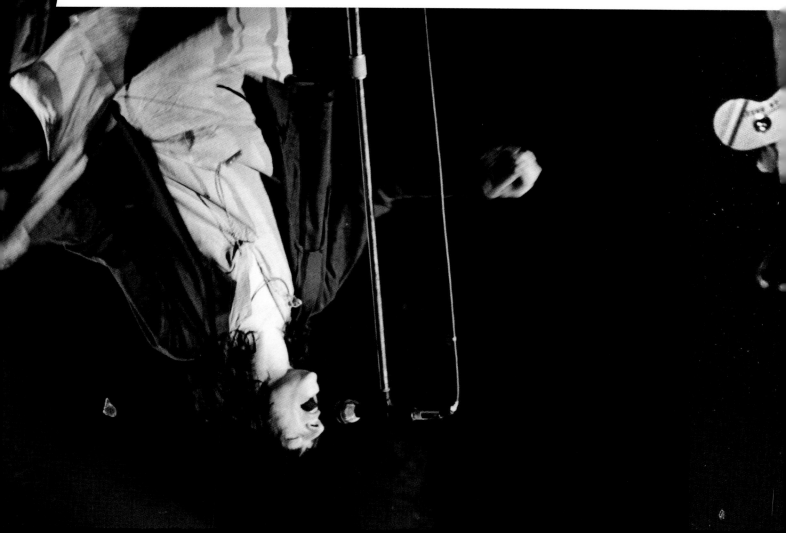

CHAPTER 4:
⚡ PUNK ROCK ⚡

THE RAMONES

Played: **PUNK ROCK**

⊸ PLAYLIST ⊸

"Blitzkrieg Bop" (1976)

"Sheena is a Punk Rocker" (1977)

'Teenage Lobotomy" (1977)

"Rockaway Beach" (1977)

"Do You Wanna Dance?" (1978)

"I Wanna Be Sedated" (1979)

"Rock and Roll High School" (1979)

"Do You Remember Rock and Roll Radio" (1980)

"Pet Sematary" (1989)

"Life's a Gas" (1995)

Cover of the April 1976 issue of Punk *magazine, featuring the Ramones in their first significant media recognition*

The Ramones were four teenagers who started a band in Queens, New York. They loved classic rock and roll music and wanted to play it loud and fast, and in the process became what most folks consider to be the first official punk rock band in the world. The band members also decided to adopt the surname of Ramone leading to a group in which no one was actually related but they appeared as a single rock unit: Joey Ramone (vocals), Johnny Ramone (guitar), Dee Dee Ramone (bass), and Tommy Ramone (drums) who was soon replaced by Marky Ramone (drums). Their music has influenced untold scores of musicians around the world, and even though it may have sounded abrasive at the time, it is now amazing to hear how tuneful their music actually is.

SONG FACTS: "SHEENA IS A PUNK ROCKER" (1977)

Written by Joey Ramone

Released on Rocket to Russia, Sire Records, August 1977

The Ramones third LP, Rocket to Russia, is about as perfect testament to rock-and-punk rock as you can ever get: fourteen songs and a total running time of only 31 minutes. That means most songs are only 2 minutes long and "Sheena" is the longest at just under three. When asked why they played such short songs, Joey Ramone used to say that they actually played long songs, but very fast. If you listen to "Sheena Is a Punk Rocker" you can hear what he means. Everything you expect from a rock and roll song is there, but it goes by incredibly quick, and it's all boiled

Because punk rock started outside of mainstream music and culture, it began to form its own subculture. Teens who were listening to the music also began an underground form of communication, talking about shows they went to see, recordings they liked, or even just good places to hang out. Eventually, these took the form of homemade magazines made by the fans of the music called fanzines! The best part is they were hand drawn and written, photocopied, and pasted together. You can make your own, and they will be just as awesome as the real ones. In fact yours will be a real one. First, you need to think about something you're a fan of. In my case, it might actually be punk rock, but you can pick whatever you like. Current musicians, older musicians—it can even be about squirrels (but I wouldn't recommend that).

You can do this on paper with pen and pencil or on the computer. Come up with a name for your fanzine and design a cover. Decide what types of articles, messages, announcements, photos, and stories you want to include. Have each family member write or create different parts of the fanzine and then put it all together. If you really feeling ambitious, you might even send it out to some folks you know.

down to the essential ingredients; no frills, no fuss, no filler. The album was produced by the drummer, Tommy Ramone.

Joey Ramone sings about a teenage girl named Sheena. All her friends are going to hang out

Punk audience, enjoying the show at CBGB's

and do things that are associated with other forms of rock and roll. They have their surfboards (surf rock), they are going to discotheques (disco), going to a go-go ('60s rock). But Sheena has to leave them behind, and she goes to New York City to become a punk rocker.

"SHEENA IS A PUNK ROCKER"

LISTENING GUIDE

This song has a great melody, with a repeated chant in the chorus. It is a lot of fun to sing along with (and despite what you might think about punk, the lyrics are totally clean). If you want to play along with Johnny and Dee Dee, the chords are really simple. Just play power chords on guitar for the verse and chorus and use the same notes for the bass guitar.

0:00 | Verse 1 | A short guitar, bass, and drums introduction leads right into the vocal section of the verse where Joey tells us the story.
To play along: C, G, C, then A, F, A, F, then the last line is C, G.

0:31 | Chorus 1 | The main lyric repeats two times.
To play along: C, F, G, and repeat eight times with the vocal and end on a final C chord.

0:53 | Postchorus | She's a punk-punk!
To play along: The cool postchorus goes F, C, G, A#, and C. At the very end you can slide between the A# and C a few times once you get good. This section serves as just enough of a musical diversion that the verse and chorus sound fresh when they come back next.

1:10 | Verse 2 | The lyrics here are really just a variation of the first verse. If you listen closely, you will notice that the entire second part of the song is just a repetition of the first part.

1:34 | Chorus 2 | Sheena is ... , Again a double chorus

1:55 | Postchorus | Push it again

2:12 | Chorus 3 and 4 | The Ramones add on two extra choruses to end the song as it fades out.

Played: **PUNK ROCK**

The Clash live in Manchester, 1978

The Clash formed in London, England, and consisted of four main members; Joe Strummer (vocals and guitar), Mick Jones (guitar), Paul Simonon (bass), and Topper Headon (drums). They were one of the most forward-reaching bands in the early British punk scene. Unlike other punk bands, who wanted to distance themselves from the past, the Clash seemed more interested in taking the music of the past and making it work within the punk rock style. Over the years, they experimented with elements of reggae, ska, Jamaican dub, funk, and even early hip hop. They also pushed the limit of punk ideals by recording several double albums—often the purview of progressive rock bands and very different from the 31-minute LPs by the Ramones.

Mick Jones

HISTORICAL FACT/SOCIAL CONNECTIONS

If we think about the Ramones establishing the basic musical framework of punk rock (fast tempo, distorted guitars, semi-shouted vocals), then we need to acknowledge the Clash as the band that fully recognized the political power that punk could have. The name of the band (created by Simonon) came from the constant headlines in the British press about the various "clashes" between different groups of people in the unstable political and social climate. The band was fueled by a leftist political ideology and a strong support for the working class. While the Sex Pistols suggested a nihilist response to the problems of the world, as heard in the shouts of "no future" in the song "God Save the Queen" (1977), the Clash frequently spoke out against the British class system, the lack of jobs in England, and issues of racism that plagued much of the United Kingdom at the time.

Joe Strummer

Written by Joe Strummer and Mick Jones

Released on CBS Records, December 1979

This song is the lead-off tune on their third album, *London Calling*. The album cover features a photograph of Simonon smashing his bass guitar on the ground, and the lettering around the edges of the cover mimics the design of Elvis Presley's first LP for RCA back in 1956. I always looked at the cover and thought that the Clash were both paying respect to rock and roll's past and also suggesting that the past had to be smashed up and started all over again every once in a while—and of course the album seems to put the Clash in the place of Elvis for the next generation.

LISTENING GUIDE

"LONDON CALLING"

Strummer wrote the lyrics to this song in response to the near disaster that occurred at the Three Mile Island nuclear power plant in Pennsylvania in 1979. The song builds on the sense of danger he saw present in the modern world and stitches together a tale of an apocalyptic "nuclear era" where things are going from bad to worse. Fascist government authority rules and zombies walk the world. London has flooded and an ice age is coming from the environmental havoc we have caused. We've run out of fuel and society is falling apart. The entire song is presented as a radio broadcast from the surviving underground. If you were going to rewrite the lyrics to this song today, what would you talk about?

0:00 | Instrumental Introduction The drums and guitar play a steady 4/4 beat. Listen to the sharp staccato edge on the guitar sound as it strums over and over, "baw, baw, baw, baw." (That's how I hear it. Feel free to use your own onomatopoeia.) The bass guitar enters playing a minor key melody.

0:21 | Verse 1 The drums, bass, and guitar move from the stark intro sound to a looser reggae groove, but without losing the feeling of intensity. There is an urgency in Joe Strummer's voice. You can believe the fear and paranoia he is singing about.

0:50 | Chorus 1 Notice that even though this functions musically as the chorus of the song, it does not feature the title of the song. That phrase is uttered at regular intervals throughout the verses of the song. The drums swing more and the guitar plays blasts of sound. The final line "I live by the river" is so powerful because it places the singer in the midst of the disaster where the river floods.

1:06 | Verse 2 Listen for the "London calling" line sung by the band in between each phrase of Strummer's vocal melody.

1:36 | Chorus 2

1:51 | Instrumental Section The instrumental section really plays up the sense of a world gone out of control. Strummer screams out animal calls that echo, and the guitar plays screeching feedback and buzzes. The drums and bass keep the beat, but even their parts fragment and break up from time to time. There is a guitar solo here that is very different from the Jimi Hendrix style of playing. This solo played by Mick Jones is much more atmospheric, and if you listen carefully, you may be able to notice that the solo is actually played backwards—that is they recorded it in the studio with Jones playing and then reversed it on the final album. Listen for the way sounds seem to fade in instead of out.

2:21 | Chorus 3
2:36 | Instrumental Section 2

2:50 | Verse 3 Goes to the end repeating the "London calling" hook. The song ends with the sound of Morse code (created by guitar feedback) as if this was one of the last transmissions from humanity.

PATTI SMITH

Played: **PUNK ROCK/ART ROCK**

─ PLAYLIST ─

"Gloria" (1976)

"Pumping (My Heart)" (1976)

"Because the Night" (1978)

"Dancing Barefoot" (1979)

"People Have the Power" (1988)

"Gone Again" (1996)

"1959" (1997)

"Glitter in Their Eyes" (2000)

"White Rabbit" (2007)

"Maria" (2012)

Patti Smith

Patti Smith and her band came out of the same New York City music scene as the Ramones. They often performed at downtown clubs like CBGB and Max's Kansas City. Smith has the distinction of being the first artist from the punk scene to be signed to a major label and reach a level of mainstream success with the album *Horses* in 1976. Because of this, many people called her the "Godmother of Punk." A number of her songs feature a vocal delivery that sounds like spoken word, such as the opening of "Gloria," but she is also able to sing with a powerful rock voice—listen to the end of the same song. Many of her works deal with what are considered to be controversial topics, and she pulls no punches in her lyrics—a true hallmark of punk rock.

HISTORICAL FACT/SOCIAL CONNECTIONS

Bands like the Jefferson Airplane and the Grateful Dead were well known for their involvement with artists and writers in the San Francisco music scene, but the same kind of crossing of disciplines was happening in New York City during the mid-1970s. Many of the musicians who lived and performed downtown were interested in how the punk rock do-it-yourself attitude could be applied to various forms of art and creativity, and as a result many of these artists collaborated on projects. While living in New York City, Smith was involved in theater, film, art, poetry, and music.

Patti Smith and Fred "Sonic" Smith

SONG FACTS: "PEOPLE HAVE THE POWER" (1988)

Written by Patti Smith and Fred Smith | Released on Arista Records, June 1988

I picked this song for a few reasons, even though it appears more than twelve years after her first album. Much of her earlier music contains profanity and intense verbal depictions (it is punk rock) and I wanted something that you could listen to with the whole family. I also wanted something

...at showcased her political activism
Because the Night" from 1978 and cowritten by Bruce Springsteen is a great
song, but it is essentially a love song).
People Have the Power" was cowritten
y Patti Smith and her husband Fred
Sonic" Smith, who had been a member
f the hard-rocking protopunk band from
etroit, the MC 5. The lyrics of the song
se biblical imagery to suggest that we
e the masters of our own destinies,
at even though it may often appear that
overnments and armies are in control,
united group of people can change the
orld. As she says, "the power
. . . to wrestle the world from fools."

RY THIS AT HOME

ith is known for her engagement with
ficult and controversial topics such
s religion, racism, sexism, and power
ruggles over issues of class in society.
ut she did more than just write and
ng about these issues. She has been
n activist for various causes over the
ears. As the song, "People Have the
ower" points out, things only change
people act. So why not use this as
spiration for your family to get out as a
oup and do something? You can even
art with something important to your
cal community. Be sure to pick a cause
at resonates with your own personal
nvictions. You could volunteer at a food
ank, help out at an educational tutoring
nter, a homeless shelter, or even a
ommunity garden. What's important to
ou? Get out and do something about it!

"PEOPLE HAVE THE POWER"

LISTENING GUIDE

0:00 | Instrumental Introduction The song starts with a sharp announcement as the snare drum plays a fast roll into the sound of the full band playing the music that we will eventually hear as the chorus. The drums play a kick and snare drum pattern that reminds us of early 1960s girl group songs. The kick plays on beats 1 and 3 and the snare plays twice on beat 2 and once on beat 4. The total sounds like 1, 2 and 3, 4.

0:15 | Verse 1 Smith's vocal melody breaks each line of lyrical text into two phrases that work as an antecedent and a consequent. The two sections complete both the lyrical thought and the musical phrase. The first part of each line is sung over a D major chord and the second part over a G major chord. The entire verse itself is divided into two eight-measure sections. Can you hear how the second eight measures build up the energy and sound?

0:46 | Prechorus In the prechorus Smith changes the mood of the song. The lyrics talk of either dreaming or waking and the chords change to reflect this movement. The progression here is F sharp minor, D major, G major, and A major. Because the F sharp minor chord is so unexpected, it feels like a major change, especially when paired with the sparser instrumentation and the mellow rhythm.

1:02 | Chorus This is written as a big sing-along chorus. If the prechorus took us by surprise and made us feel unstable, then the chorus fully returns to solid ground. The four-measure chord progression is almost the same as the verse with an extension: D major, G major, E minor, and A major. The chorus is twelve measures long. It features eight measures of singing (the chord progression played twice) and then repeats the progression one more time as an instrumental.

1:24 | Verse 2 The music makes another shift in energy as it enters the verse. The instruments play softer so that we, once again, focus our listening on the lyrics.

1:54 | Prechorus

2:10 | Chorus

2:32 | Verse 3 This verse starts with an extended musical section that comes out of the instrumental. It functions as a transition and creates anticipation for the lyrics.

3:09 | Prechorus

3:26 | Triple Chorus (sort of) This chorus is three times as long as the previous ones, but it also does away with the four measures of the instrumental that we normally have at the end of each chorus. So, in actuality, it is only twenty-four measures long—the eight measures of lyrics repeated three times. In the third part, Smith introduces a new melody as she expands on her message.

4:10 | Triple Chorus Almost the same as the last triple chorus, except that this time Smith changes the order of the three sections so that the new melody plays in the middle eight measures. This is a good idea because it allows the last eight measures of the song to repeat the sing-along chorus melody.

TALKING HEADS

Played: **POSTPUNK/ART ROCK/NEW WAVE**

⌐ PLAYLIST ⌐

"Love → Building on Fire" (1977)

"Psycho Killer" (1977)

"Take Me to the River" (1978)

"Life During Wartime" (1979)

"Once in a Lifetime" (1980)

"Houses in Motion" (1980)

"Burning Down the House" (1983)

"And She Was" (1985)

"Wild Wild Life" (1986)

"(Nothing) But Flowers" (1988)

The Talking Heads perform at CBGB, 1977

The Talking Heads were a part of the New York City punk explosion and even played their first official gig as the opening band for the Ramones at CBGB. The group featured three talented musicians who had attended the Rhode Island School of Design together, David Byrne (vocals, guitar), Chris Frantz (drums), and Tina Weymouth (bass, vocals). After releasing their first single, "Love → Building on Fire," they added Jerry Harrison (guitar, keyboards). The group represents the transition from guitar-oriented punk rock to a more expansive sound that was eventually called postpunk or new wave.

TRY THIS AT HOME

The East Village in New York City is not what it used to be—it's actually much nicer. Having said that, much of what the Village was when the punk bands came about is gone, but you can still walk around the same streets where CBGBs and Max's Kansas City used to be. The area still has a lineage the punk days, so if you look hard enough you might still be able to find stores like Trash and Vaudeville, and the New York University campus keeps it feeling very youthful. The Village has always been home to good food and record stores (even now), so make sure to look for some of those as well.

HISTORICAL FACT/SOCIAL CONNECTIONS

From the concert film Stop Making Sense, *1984*

The band members' art school background played a big part in the sound and vision of the group. The Talking Heads experimented with adding avant-garde ideas (synthesizers and noise sounds) and world music (afrobeat and Latin music) into the punk sound. They were also one of the early rock groups to pioneer the use of performance art multimedia, and video as an important part of their live shows. This helped the band become a mainstream sensation when their humorous and creative music videos such as "Burning Down the House" found a home on the fledgling MTV network in the early 1980s.

SONG FACTS: "LIFE DURING WARTIME" (1979)

Written by David Byrne, Chris Frantz, Jerry Harrison, and Tina Weymouth

Released on Sire Records, 1979

By looking at the lyrics of this song, we can see the development of a particular theme in punk rock—the vision of an apocalyptic future as commentary on current conditions, much like "London Calling" by the Clash. This song from the Talking Heads' third album presents a worst-case scenario of life in the modern city where day-to-day life has become kind of warfare. During the late 1970s the Alphabet City part of New York City was a mess, and Byrne wrote this song while thinking about what could happen if everything really fell apart. There are some other interesting similarities to the Clash. In "London Calling", the Clash sing about the death of what they called phony Beatlemania, meaning that the hype about punk was over and now it was time to start doing something other than talking about it. In "Life During Wartime," David Byrne makes a similar suggestion when he mentions that the days of the Mudd Club and CBGB were now behind them, and they were moving into a new space—musically and personally.

LISTENING GUIDE

"LIFE DURING WARTIME"

Musically, this song draws a lot of inspiration from the structure of soul music songs we listened to in chapter 3. There are only two basic sections to the song—a verse and a chorus. These two musical grooves repeat over and over as Byrne tells his story over the top. In this way, it is also like Patti Smith's early experiments with spoken word and music. If you listen carefully, you can hear lots of little variations in how the instruments play the basic riffs. The funny thing is that, despite the rather bleak lyrics, the song is really fun to dance around the house to. So, if you have some young kids in the house, feel free to just dance around and sing, "This ain't no fooling around" at the top of your lungs.

0:00 | Instrumental Introduction The song opens with eight measures of bass, drums, guitar, and keyboards. The synthesizer plays a nasal tone that sounds a little bit like an electronic horn section while the electric guitar plays a rhythmic countermelody.

0:15 | Verse 1 David Byrne has a unique vocal timbre that perfectly presents the pent-up paranoia present in the lyrics. His delivery moves effortlessly back and forth between a spoken dialogue style in the verse and a high-pitched melodic delivery in the chorus.

0:43 | Chorus Byrne sings the famous "This ain't no party" lyric. Listen to the instrumentation. All the same parts are playing, but in the chorus they play longer notes, and thus create a more static texture. This helps to highlight Byrne's frantic delivery.

0:58 | Verse 2 The lyrics at the end of this verse start to get pretty dark, even though Byrne's vocal style is emotionally pretty consistent with the previous verse. He suggests that he goes out to work in the nighttime (true in his case as a musician), and that he might never get home in this urban war zone.

1:26 | Chorus

1:41 | Guitar Solo This guitar solo is really great, mostly because it's barely a guitar solo at all. Harrison just strums one note on the upbeats over and over. The high-pitched sounds cuts right though the mix of the other instruments, but after a few strokes, it feels like it just falls in with the rhythm of all the other instruments.

1:56 | Verse 3 The screeching electric guitar continues into the verse as Byrne sings about how the problem is happening in cities all over the United States, not just New York. I really like the kind of obsessed details he adds to the lyrics, like the fact that he is storing up peanut butter to survive for a few days in case of emergency.

2:25 | Chorus

2:40 | Verse 4 Byrne mentions that the survivors in his story dress like students and housewives, or in a suit or tie. In other words these folks are us, we are all moving toward this strange future state. Byrne keeps singing as the song fades out, and the music never makes a final return to the chorus. The story has no ending. One of the last things we clearly hear him say is that he has burned up all his notebooks because they won't help him survive in the wasteland.

THE REPLACEMENTS

Played: **PUNK ROCK/POST PUNK/ALTERNATIVE ROCK**

— PLAYLIST —

"Takin' a Ride" (1981)

"Hootenanny" (1983)

"Color Me Impressed" (1983)

"I Will Dare" (1984)

"Unsatisfied" (1984)

"Hold My Life" (1987)

"Can't Hardly Wait" (1987)

"Alex Chilton" (1987)

"I'll Be You" (1989)

"Merry Go Round" (1990)

The Replacements on SNL, *1986 (l to r: Tommy Stinson, Chris Mars, Paul Westerberg, and Bob Stinson)*

All the other bands discussed in this chapter come from New York City or London, but this last band formed in the Midwest of the United States in 1979. For kids like the Stinson brothers who grew up in Minneapolis, Minnesota, punk rock came to them side by side with the sounds of '70s rock. This meant that they listened to the Rolling Stones, the Beatles, and Big Star side by side with the Ramones, the Clash, and the Damned. The band featured Bob Stinson (guitar), Tommy Stinson (bass), Paul Westerberg (vocals, guitar), and Chris Mars (drums). Westerberg turned out to be a masterful songwriter, and many of the band's early songs featured interesting interpretations of typical teenage boy problems.

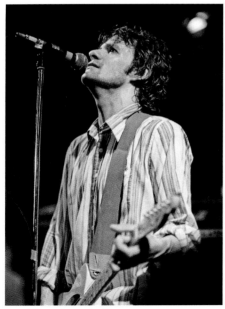

Paul Westerberg, 1987

SONG FACTS: "I WILL DARE" (1984)

Written by Paul Westerberg

Released on Twin/Tone Records, July 1984

This song was the first single from the band's 1984 album *Let It Be* (an obvious reference to the Beatles album of the same name). Peter Buck of the band R.E.M. plays guitar on the song (more about that band in chapter 7). The lyrics of the song are a great example of Westerberg's ability

"I Will Dare"

LISTENING GUIDE

The overall sound of the song is somewhat abrasive when you put it next to the polished pop music of the 1980s. For example, compare it to the hit song "Sister Christian" by Night Ranger from the same year. I know that's a ridiculous comparison, but that's the point. Let's not forget how different punk music was at the time. On the other hand, "I Will Dare" is much more tuneful and melodic when we compare it to other punk rock. The drum's shuffle rhythm keeps the tune bounding along in a happy stride. This song is a good example of how the early punk sound was altered by bands like the Replacements when they mixed it up with '70s classic rock.

0:00 | Instrumental Introduction The jangling clean guitar sound opens the song along with the hi-hats of the drum kit for the first four measures. Then the bass and the full drum kit enter for the next eight measures.

0:18 | Verse 1 The introduction music continues as Westerberg begins to sing. There is a brief instrumental break at the end of the verse when you can hear that the main guitar changes its strumming pattern.

0:33 | Verse 2

0:45 | Chorus The guitar pattern that was the focus of the verse music changes to a picked melody with some slight distortion. The drums and bass change into a classic walking pattern as the bass moves up and down the scale. This has a very different feel from the verse music.

0:57 | Verse 3 The two-verse structure from the opening of the song is collapsed into a single section this time.

1:26 | Chorus This time, they double the length of the chorus, a common songwriting technique. The idea is that once we know the hook, the main melody, we will want to hear more of it.

1:48 | Guitar Solo The solo here is ever so slightly out of tune with the rest of the band, but it actually just seems to add some extra spice to the song. Besides, a slightly out-of-tune guitar is not really a problem in punk rock.

2:13 | Instrumental Break (with mandolin)

2:18 | Verse 4 At the end of this verse, the lyrics just drift away and the music continues.

2:44 | Chorus

to make teen boredom and angst sound like poetry. The song opens with a series of questions that Westerberg seems to be asking a girl. At least I think that's what he's talking about. As it turns out, the lyrics contain no information about the other person in the song, it's just Westerberg's side of the conversation. Also, we can make a guess about what he will dare to do—I always think that he is taking a chance on a relationship with the girl—but the song never actually says that either.

TRY THIS AT HOME

Now it's your turn to write a punk song. As you've now learned, the music can be very straightforward (the Ramones) or mix up a bunch of new ideas (the Clash and the Talking Heads). That means you can work on writing a song if you don't know how to play very well (most punk musicians learned to play while in a band), or you can do something really awesome if you have some skill. Don't have any idea what chords to use? Here, I'll give you three: C, F, G (by the way, if you just play them as open power chords then that's actually the chorus of the Ramones' "Sheena Is a Punk Rocker"). Remember, it should be fast—but it doesn't have to be. It should have a lot of repeated strumming on an electric guitar—but it doesn't have to. The lyrics can be a political statement about the world like Patti Smith, or it can be something very intimate, like the Replacements. But it should have some kind of attitude—it is punk after all. Now most of all, just go do it.

CHAPTER 5:

DANCE M

SIC

LAB 31

MICHAEL JACKSON

Played: **POP**

⌐ PLAYLIST ⌐

"Don't Stop 'til You Get Enough" (1979)

"Rock with You" (1979)

"Beat It" (1982)

"Billie Jean" (1982)

"Thriller" (1982)

"Bad" (1987)

"Man in the Mirror" (1987)

"Remember the Time" (1991)

"Black or White" (1991)

"You Are Not Alone" (1995)

"You Rock My World" (2001)

"Butterflies" (2001)

Michael Jackson and his producer Quincy Jones

It's amazing to see how popular Michael Jackson is all over the world. Even though the majority of his solo music was released in the 1980s and 1990s, those songs are still as powerful today a when he recorded them. Michael (1958–2009) was born in Gary, Indiana, and started singing with his brothers at the age of six. The Jackson Five went on to be one of the most successful bands ever recorded at Motown Records in Detroit with hit songs like, "I Want You Back," and "ABC." When Michael went solo in 1975, he began a relationship with music producer Quincy Jones, and they went on to create some of the most popular records of the twentieth century. Jackson was not only a great singer, he was also an amazing performer who brought elements of dance, theater, and fashion into his work. He revolutionized the format of the music video on the fledgling MTV cable channel, and eventually went on to earn the nickname, "The King of Pop."

SONG FACTS: "BILLIE JEAN" (1982)

Written by Michael Jackson

Released on Thriller, Epic Records, November 1982

"Billie Jean" is an important song for a number of reasons. It was the second single released from the *Thriller* album, and it became a major hit. The music video was one of the first major

RY THIS AT HOME

...his is your chance to become an MTV
...usic video star (or YouTube sensation).
...ke out your cell phone and take turns
...ning each other lip-syncing to your
...vorite songs, and then sit down and
...atch them back to back.

...ant to be more serious about your
...iance at video stardom? Assign each
...rson in the house a different job.
...omeone needs to come up with the
...eo concept. Someone will need to
...sign the sets and create the dance
...oreography. You have to have a
...ector, and most of all the performers.
...an it out and see if you can come up
...th a number of different shots and
...kes, and then put them all into video
...iting software to cut together your
...rfect video. Have you been performing
...usic at home? Maybe you're all set to
...n a video of your family actually playing
...e music as a band.

"BILLIE JEAN"

LISTENING GUIDE

Lyrically, Jackson is singing about a paternity suit about a woman named Billie Jean who claims her child belongs to the singer (Fun fact: the character Billie Jean is also mentioned in the lyrics of the first song on *Thriller*, "Wanna Be Startin' Somethin'.").

It's funny that when I listened to this song when it came out in 1982, I never really thought too much about the words because the melody, rhythm, and Jackson's dancing always drew my attention away from the words. The arrangement of the instruments and the voice is beautiful. Listen to how many versions of Jackson's voice are present in the song. Through the magic of multitrack recording, he sings the main melody and the backing vocals along with all the uhs, whoos, and ahhs that punctuate the soundscape like a percussion instrument.

0:00 | Introduction | I always say that truly great pop songs grab you from the very first seconds that you hear them. The drum beat that opens "Billie Jean" does that. It has a swagger, a stride. You know it's "Billie Jean" right away. Even the actual sound made by the drums is unique. Once the drum beat is established, new instruments enter one at a time. First, we hear Michael producing some rhythmic sounds, then that classic bass line enters, and just before the verse, the strings.

0:30 | Verse 1 | Each verse in this song has a refrain at the end—a short lyric and melody that is the same each time, "Gonna dance, on the floor...."

0:54 | Verse 2

1:10 | Prechorus | The prechorus changes both the musical progression and the mood of the song. When Michael sings "People always told me..." the music begins to build up and create a sense of tension that will lead into the chorus.

1:27 | Chorus | In this song, the music of the chorus is both a release of the tension we felt in the section before and a great hook that makes you want to sing along.

Listen carefully and you can hear how detailed the arrangement is. Rhythmic guitar parts and several keyboard melodies are different from the main vocal melody.

1:51 | Verse 3 | New keyboard parts add a new flavor to this verse so it never feels like an exact repetition of verse 1 and 2.

2:16 | Verse 4
2:32 | Prechorus
2:48 | Chorus

3:05 | Chorus | The chorus repeats with some additional instrumentation to build it up.

3:30 | Break | Don't forget that this is a dance song, so that break allows the main groove of the music to take center stage. It also features Michael's signature "heees" and "whoos." At 3:45, there is reference to the chorus at the end of the section as the vocals sing "the kid is not my son" before the music moves back into the actual chorus.

3:54 | Chorus | The chorus material, or a variation of it, continues for the rest of the song and fades out just before the 5 minute mark.

‑ PLAYLIST ‑

"Mighty Mighty" (1974)

"Shining Star" (1975)

"That's the Way of the World" (1975)

"Serpentine Fire" (1977)

"Got to Get You into My Life" (1978)

"September" (1978)

"Boogie Wonderland" (1979)

"After the Love Has Gone" (1979)

"Let's Groove" (1981)

"System of Survival" (1987)

Earth, Wind & Fire live

Earth, Wind & Fire

Earth, Wind & Fire (EWF) was started in Chicago, Illinois, in 1969 by singer and songwriter Maurice White. Innovators of a new dance music sound for the 1970s, it featured a number of musicians (including a big horn section) playing a fusion of R&B, soul, and funk. Earth, Wind & Fire owed a lot to the music of James Brown, but also brought in elements of '60s soul music like the Isley Brothers, and the psychedelic soul of Sly and the Family Stone. The result was a musical sound that served as the basic model for disco bands later in the '70s. Classic EWF featured Maurice White singing a dual lead with Philip Bailey. During their live concerts they performed to sold-out crowds with a stage show that was based on White's interest in Egyptology.

HISTORICAL FACT/SOCIAL CONNECTIONS

Take a moment and stop to think about the way that musical sounds and styles interact with each other. When rock and roll first began in the late 1940s and early 1950s, it was really a mixture of many different American music styles. When rock and roll found its way over to England and came back to the United States as part of the British Invasion, it had new elements added to it from its journey. During the 1970s, the music began to split into many different particular sounds (disco, punk, arena rock), but it is important to remember that most of those styles we created through a

"SEPTEMBER"

SONG FACTS: "SEPTEMBER" (1978)

Written by Maurice White, Al McKay, and Allee Willis

Released on Columbia Records, November 1978

I have a personal admission to make—I can't help but feel good and dance when I hear this song. From a songwriting point of view, it is quite amazing and the perfect example of how lyrics can work even if they don't make much sense. The song is about feeling good and falling in love, but what is Philip Bailey actually singing in the chorus? For years, I thought it was everything from "all and" to "on and on" and sometimes even "party on!" Turns out he's just saying "ba de ya" as an exuberant statement of feeling good. And, man, does that work. I love the sound of the intricate vocal harmony on the extended chorus at the end of the song.

mixture of things that came before it. In the case of Earth, Wind & Fire, they were using little bits and pieces of everything they heard in black music up to that moment (in fact White had even been a session player over at Chess Records in Chicago), and they were creating a sound that would become the basis for disco at the end of the decade. Have your family think about these relationships and how most all artists take something from the past to make something new.

The song is in a major key and most of the chords use an added 7th note above the root of the chord in the harmony. For example, if the root note is D, then the D7 chord would have the notes D, F sharp, A, and C. You can also have a major chord with a major 7th note above it; a Dmaj7 has the notes D, F sharp, A and C sharp.

In "September", the 7th chords give the music a full and luxurious sound. The song is also very rhythmic—in a way similar to funk music—with each instrument playing its own short motive and adding to the total sound of the song. Just listen to the opening 20 seconds for a good example of this. Throughout the song, the bass line is always moving, playing up and down the scale while it is locked in sync with the drums.

0:00 | Introduction Listen closely to all the instruments and the short little ideas they play in this opening:
Guitar: a short rhythmic melody.
Rhythm guitar—a jangling background rhythm on just two notes
Cowbell: plays straight on the main beat. The kick drum plays this same beat when it enters.
Shaker: a steady rhythm twice as fast as the pulse.
Piano: a series of 7th chords in the low register and some accent notes in the upper register

The horns and bass enter only in the last section to transition to the verse.

0:20 | Verse 1 Most of the instruments play the same motives they established in the introduction, and the addition of the bass really pushes the song along. The horns only play in the last measure of this section.

0:35 | Verse 2 The instrumentation builds up with the addition of a string section that plays its own melody in the background.

0:50 | Chorus 1 Philip Bailey's lead here in a high falsetto voice adds a nice sense of contrast to White's deeper tenor voice in the verses. The horns play a counter melody in the background that is a great bit of musical foreshadowing because it becomes the main melody in the next section.

1:06 | Postchorus Various instrumental groups and the vocalists perform short motives as if they were all horn instruments. The vocalists all sing, "ba-di-da-ba-do," which is the counter melody from the chorus.

1:21 | Verse 3
1:36 | Verse 4
1:51 | Chorus 2 (repeats two times)

2:22 | Bridge The backing instruments don't change much here. Many of them play the same motives that they have been playing all along—for example, the guitar is playing its melody from the introduction and the horns are playing their melody from the postchorus. But the new combination of parts and the addition of the new vocal melody create a feeling of departure. It's not enough to disturb the groove, but it is enough to mix things up.

2:37 | Chorus 3 (repeats four times) The horn section in the final repetition of the chorus sounds like it is playing too hard. There are just a few subtle cracks in the high notes. I actually love these because I think that it adds to the overall exuberance of the song, as if the whole thing can barely be contained in the grooves of the record.

- PLAYLIST -

"Dance, Dance, Dance (Yowsah, Yowsah, Yowsah)" (1977)

"Everybody Dance" (1977)

"Le Freak" (1978)

"I Want Your Love" (1978)

"My Feet Keep Dancing" (1979)

"Good Times" (1979)

"Rebels Are We" (1980)

"Real People" (1980)

"Stage Fright" (1981)

"Give Me the Lovin'" (1983)

Chic perform live, 1979

Chic formed in 1976 in New York City and featured the talents of guitarist Nile Rodgers and bass player Bernard Edwards (1952–1996). Their music let us hear how the music of funk- and R&B–inspired bands like Earth, Wind & Fire gave way to a new and original disco sound at the end of the 1970s. Chic used funky rhythms and catchy melodic hooks, but Edwards and Rodgers' skill as producers allowed them to create a minimalist approach to their arrangements with the goal of connecting the music directly to the dance floor. In fact, Edwards and Rodgers often wrote songs thinking about how they might sound when they were played in budding disco clubs in New York City like the famous Studio 54. Because the pure disco sound started to disappear in the early 1980s, the group disbanded in 1983 and both Rodgers and Edwards went on to successful careers as songwriters and producers for other musicians.

Chic, 1977 (l to r: Bernard Edwards, Norma Jean Wright, Nile Rodgers, and Tony Thompson)

HISTORICAL FACT/SOCIAL CONNECTIONS

The musical term disco actually comes from the name of the places where the music was originally played. Starting in the late 1950s, a number of nightclubs in France began to feature music played on record instead of traditional live musicians. These clubs were called discothèques—essentially translated as music library, or maybe more appropriately as record club. The term quickly caught on and by the mid-1960s in the United States the name was shortened to disco. Many of these

Studio 54, 1975

clubs played some variation of black dance music (such as Earth, Wind & Fire or the O'Jays). The heyday of disco came in the late 1970s when major cities like Miami, Los Angeles, and New York featured large disco clubs with multiple rooms, famous DJs, and lines out the door to get in. By far, the most famous was Studio 54, located at 254 West 54th Street in New York City. The club was also known for the clientele it drew, including Mick Jagger, Andy Warhol, Michael Jackson, and Calvin Klein. It's amazing to think that at the same time in the late '70s, just fifty blocks south in New York City, the punk club CBGB was hosting bands like the Ramones.

SONG FACTS: "GOOD TIMES" (1979)

Written by Bernard Edwards and Nile Rodgers

Released on Atlantic Records, 1979

One of the interesting things about this song is the positive nature of the lyrics, considering the fact that the late '70s were not really good times. Unemployment was high, there was a gas shortage, New York City was on the verge of bankrupcy, and the country was still recovering from a torment of the Vietnam War. But what Edwards and Rodgers advocate here is for the listener to put all of those concerns aside and let the music put you in a new state of mind—to make your time on the dance floor at the disco a transformative experience.

TRY THIS AT HOME

Trying your hand at being a DJ in the "old days" was not so easy to do. A disco DJ would have to use two turntables with two records and beat match the albums to make sure that they worked together. Then they would have to fade from one record the next. The DJ also had to think about when to set a mood of the party, such as when to play a series of fast songs or when to slow things down with a ballad. Today, you will have to make good artistic choices (if you want people to listen and dance), but the physical action of DJing has become much easier—especially if you have an iPad or iPhone. Go download one of the many DJ apps. Now you can download songs from your own digital library and try ing for yourself.

"GOOD TIMES"

LISTENING GUIDE

I want you to find and listen to the original 12-inch (30.5 cm) dance record version of this song (it's just over 8 minutes long). In the 1970s, a song like this might be released on an LP with one mix, and then also have a shorter version made for a 45 rpm release, and another longer one made for dance clubs called the 12-inch mix—because it was released on a full-size vinyl record even though it might feature only one or two songs on a side. The 12-inch mix records also had an added bonus. The smaller number of grooves on the record boosted the bass sounds, which was perfect for dance music.

0:00 | Introduction The song begins by establishing the basic elements of the song. The jingly rhythm guitar, the melodic bass line, the piano chords, and the steady four-on-the-floor bass line (in which the kick drum plays on every beat of a 4/4 measure).

0:18 | Chorus Once the instruments have set the groove, the vocalists enter singing the hook, "Good times."

0:53 | Verse 1 The string section begins to play another melody in the background. If you listen carefully you will notice that it does not play all the time.

1:27 | Chorus Same as the first chorus except that the string section melody from the first verse continues to play.

2:02 | Verse 2

2:37 | Chorus

3:12 | Breakdown After a strong flourish from the string section, the majority of instruments drop out and the song focuses entirely on the bass guitar and the drums (which strongly feature the handclap on the backbeat). This part of the song was entirely conceived by Edwards and Rodgers for the dance floor. In this section, the DJ could either let the groove ride or even mix in elements of other songs from another 12-inch (30.5 cm) record.

It is almost a full minute before the song begins to slowly build back up. First, the digital piano sound enters at 4:04, playing the same chords that the piano played in the opening introduction. At 4:40, that piano enters playing a more rhythmic version of the same chord progression. At 5:14, (two minutes into the break) the electric guitar reenters, and at 5:30, the drums begin to build up the rhythmic pattern in the hi hats.

This is the most famous part of this song (partially because it is the section that is always sampled by hip hop musicians).

6:04 | Verse There is a totally smooth transition back into the final verse of the song.

6:38 | Chorus The final chorus is a jam that takes us all the way to the end of the song.

DONNA SUMMER

Played: **DISCO/RHYTHM AND BLUES/POP**

⊸ PLAYLIST ⊸

"Love to Love You Baby" (1975)

"I Feel Love" (1977)

"Last Dance" (1978)

"MacArthur Park" (1978)

"Hot Stuff" (1979)

"Dim All the Lights" (1979)

"On the Radio" (1980)

"State of Independence" (1982)

"She Works Hard for the Money" (1983)

"When Love Cries" (1991)

"Fame (The Game)" (2008)

Donna Summer, 1976

Donna Summer (1948–2012) was often called the "Queen of Disco," and while I think it is a fitting moniker for a woman who established the sound and image of the disco queen, I also think that the name tends to overshadow her ability to sing and write songs outside of the disco style. Born and raised in Boston, Massachusetts, Summer started like so many other singers of the time by performing in her church choir. It was during the early 1970s, when she was performing in the Munich, Germany–based production of the musical *Hair* that she met producer Giorgio Moroder. The two launched a successful collaboration that lasted until 1980 and produced numerous disco hits including the 17-minute disco fantasy "Love to Love You Baby." During the 1980s and beyond, Summer demonstrated her ability to sing and write songs in various styles including rock, new wave, and pop.

HISTORICAL FACT/SOCIAL CONNECTIONS

The analog synthesizer is an instrument that uses analog circuits and oscillators to put together elemental parts and generate a new sound. Ideas for such an instrument date back to the early twentieth century (such as the Teleharmonium and the Ondes Martenot), and by the 1950s room-size instruments were able to produce complex sounds from a series of instructions, such as the RCA Mark II. In 1963, inventor Robert Moog met musician Herbert Deutsch and, together, they spent the next year developing the use of voltage-controlled oscillators to make a more user-friendly analog synthesizer. The result was the Moog synthesizer. Musicians flocked to it for its ease of use and its ability to produce exciting new electronic sounds.

Bob Moog and the Moog Synthesizer

SONG FACTS: "I FEEL LOVE" (1977)

Written by Donna Summer, Giorgio Moroder, and Pete Bellotte

Released on Casablanca Records, July 1977

In 1977 Donna Summer, Pete Bellotte, and Giorgio Moroder worked together to write a song that would take Summer's gospel and rock background and unite it with the fully synthesized

...nna Summer and Giorgio Moroder

TRY THIS AT HOME

...this song intrigues you, it's time to find a Moog synthesizer and try it yourself. Is it possible to buy an original Moog synthesizer like the Mini Moog and try the real thing, but it might be rather expensive. The original items can be hard program if you're new to synthesizers. I suggest you go and download the Animoog app onto your iPad. This app made by the Moog company and lets you create and record your sounds. If you enjoy working with this one, there are many other software synths available online. Some of them will even run on a PC or laptop, so you can program your own synthesizer no matter where you are.

LISTENING GUIDE

"I FEEL LOVE"

0:00 | Introduction The song begins with a swirling, held out, synthesizer chord. Imagine hearing this in a dance club back in 1977 when such sounds were not commonplace. It may have sounded like a sound from the future—which is actually what the songwriters wanted.

A number of new sounds then enter simultaneously while the swirling synth continues to play: a thumping bassline, an arpeggiated chord, a new buzzing melodic line, and the sounds of a kick drum, snare drum, and hi hats. All of these sounds are being made by a single Moog synthesizer. This may seem like nothing special today, but to produce this intricate rhythmic track would have taken a painstaking amount of work in 1977. Each sound had to be recorded separately and synced together using tape recording equipment.

0:42 | Verse The synthesized background continues as Summer begins to sing her vocal melody. Can you hear which synthesized elements continue to play and which ones stop in the verse? How might you describe some of the new sounds that are added? How do they change over time? You might also notice that reverb is added to Summer's voice to make her sound like she is in a large space.

1:27 | Chorus Summer recorded her voice multiple times in order to make it sound like a full group of singers. The synthesized chords from the opening return to fill out the sound.

1:58 | Verse 2 Summer's voice sings two different versions of the melody in this verse—much like Marvin Gaye's voice in "What's Going On."

2:43 | Chorus

3:00 | Break Like so many other dance songs, "I Feel Love" features a break to be used by the DJ on the dance floor. This one begins in a really inventive way as the sound of the chorus fades out. This song actually replicates the feeling of a DJ mixing into a new song during the fade-out of an old one. I imagine that many people on the dance floor were fooled into thinking that the Donna Summer song had actually ended when they first heard this.

In my opinion, this is one of the funkiest synthesized grooves ever created. I love the electronic white noise bursts that are used to simulate the handclaps of songs like Chic's "Good Times."

4:05 | Verse 3 As is common in many disco songs, the last verse seems to simply "appear" out of the midst of the break.

4:50 | Chorus The final chorus fades again and sounds a lot like the one that came at the start of the break. But then the pulsing synthesizers fade as well to end the song, just shy of 6 minutes.

THE BEE GEES

Played: **SOFT ROCK /RHYTHM AND BLUES /DISCO**

PLAYLIST

"New York Mining Disaster 1941" (1967)

"To Love Somebody" (1967)

"I Started a Joke" (1968)

"How Can You Mend a Broken Heart" (1971)

"Jive Talkin'" (1975)

"Nights on Broadway" (1975)

"You Should Be Dancing" (1976)

"How Deep Is Your Love" (1977)

"Stayin' Alive" (1977)

"Night Fever" (1977)

"Tragedy" (1979)

"One" (1989)

The Bee Gees, 1975

The Bee Gees became massive superstars in the late 1970s, so it might surprise you to find out that they actually started as a band in 1958. The group featured three brothers who were originally from England, but grew up in Queensland, Australia: Barry Gibb (b. 1946), Robin Gibb (1949–2012), and Maurice Gibb (1949–2003). Early on, they performed rock and roll, but by the mid-1960s they became an international sensation with their lush vocal harmonies fronting a soft rock sound with just a touch of folk rock. At the time, many critics compared their outstanding vocal ability to the Beatles. The band then made a major shift when they began to experiment with American dance music and disco with the help of famed producer Arif Mardin. In 1977, the brothers wrote and recorded much of the music on the soundtrack for the film *Saturday Night Fever*—an album that made them one of the best-selling groups of all time.

From the film Saturday Night Fever

HISTORICAL FACT/SOCIAL CONNECTIONS

The 1977 film *Saturday Night Fever* stars John Travolta as a young man who pushes aside the difficulties of his everyday life to become a superstar on the disco club dance floor on the weekends. The film features a number of beautifully choreographed and filmed dance scenes— and for many Americans, this may have been the first time they ever glimpsed the dance moves and culture of a disco club including the lit-up dance floor! The movie helped to make disco a household term, and pushed a musical sound that was rooted in black bands and gay nightclubs to a wider audience. Suddenly, every hotel and airport bar flaunted a disco night, trying to draw people into the scene. In many ways, this quick ascension into the mainstream was one of the major contributions to the decline of disco just a few years later.

Barry Gibb, 1979

SONG FACTS:
"STAYIN' ALIVE" (1977)

Written by Barry Gibb, Robin Gibb, and Maurice Gibb

Released on RSO, December 1977

...he brothers wrote this song specifically ...r the soundtrack of *Saturday Night ...ver*, but at the time they didn't know ...hat the plot of the film was. Yet, the tune ...oes a great job of capturing the spirit of ...e movie and the situation the characters ...nd themselves in. The way it is used in ...e opening credits of the film is one of the ...est uses of music that I've ever seen. The ...e lyric that always grabs my attention ...in the chorus, "feel the city breakin' ...nd everybody shakin'," it both captures ...e fact that the city is falling apart and ...e idea that people are dancing the ...jes away. It's also possible to hear the ...oreakin'" as a reference to hip hop in the ...onx where people were break dancing ...the sound of DJs on the streets.

RY THIS AT HOME

...you have been doing all of the activities ...o far, then you've already made your ...wn psychedelic club at home in the ...yle of the UFO club (back in Lab 17). ...ow, it is time to turn on the disco fever. ...ou'll need to decorate with lots of shiny ...rfaces and get a strobe light and a ...sco ball. Have someone in your family ...lunteer to be the DJ. The tunes don't ...ave to be disco songs. Maybe you can ...ix up some classic disco tunes listed ...this book with some newer songs that ...apture the same sound. Then invite ...ome friends over and it's time to boogie ...n down. Fruit juice smoothies make for a ...eat cool down after dancing.

"STAYIN' ALIVE"

LISTENING GUIDE

This song has three things going for it. One, it has a killer groove created by looping a drum part on a tape recorder. Two, it has a very catchy melody that sticks in your head, even if you can't hear all the words. And three, it has a beautiful arrangement that packs a ton of music into a small space but never feels overcrowded. Listen several times and try to hear all the parts playing in the background.

0:00 | Instrumental Introduction Like most disco-era dance songs, "Stayin' Alive" lays a lot of the elements on the table right at the beginning. The four-on-the-floor drumbeat serves as the foundation with a funky bass line and auxiliary percussion playing over the top. An electric guitar and an acoustic guitar play strummed chords and a digital piano plays a series of syncopated chords. A string section that will be featured more fully later is used to create accents and tension in the opening.

0:14 | Verse 1 Barry Gibb came up with a new singing style in the early 1970s when the band first began to play dance music. His full falsetto voice sits in a very high register and yet he still has an amazing amount of control.

0:24 | Prechorus The bass line stalls out and the string section swells to create tension as Barry's voice is joined by his brothers.

0:33 | Chorus The music actually reduces the energy level from the prechorus allowing the vocals' rapid-fire melody to come back front and center. The three brothers sing together in perfect harmony.

The chorus ends with the vocals taking center stage as the Gibbs hold out a long descending melody on the word "alive."

0:59 | Verse 2 Same as verse 1 but with new added strings.

1:12 | Prechorus

1:22 | Chorus This time, the Bee Gees keep the energy level of the chorus high by adding a new melody in the string section. During the "ah, ah, ah" vocal section, the strings even play the same melody on the off beats in between each "ah."

1:47 | Bridge A new melody in the vocal with an added horn section.

2:15 | Verse 3

2:24 | Prechorus

2:33 | Chorus

2:59 | Bridge The same musical material as the previous bridge. It now serves as the jam to end the song, and as the music continues there is more new material from the horns and strings. The brothers Gibb ad lib lines over the music as it fades out.

MADONNA

Played: **DANCE MUSIC / POP**

– PLAYLIST –

"Everybody" (1982)

"Holiday" (1983)

"Lucky Star" (1984)

"Material Girl" (1984)

"Into the Groove" (1985)

"Open Your Heart" (1986)

"Who's That Girl" (1987)

"Express Yourself" (1989)

"Vogue" (1990)

"Ray of Light" (1998)

"Music" (2000)

"Give Me All Your Luvin'" (2012)

Madonna performs live, 1988

If Michael Jackson was the King of Pop during the 1980s and 1990s, then there can be little doubt that Madonna was the queen. The singer, dancer, songwriter, producer, and businesswoman broke so many of the molds the record industry set for her that it is hard to list them all here. She pushed the boundaries of what was acceptable subject matter in her lyrics (sex, religion, female empowerment), and her music videos took it a step beyond that. Many people were outraged by her confident persona and her constant use of role reversals to put women in a place of power. The sound of her music was firmly rooted in early '80s pop—a sound that had strong roots in the disco and electronic dance music of the '70s. She has continued to evolve her musical sound and public image over the years, demonstrating an amazing ability to tap into current trends and make them her own.

HISTORICAL FACT/SOCIAL CONNECTIONS

Madonna is an important artist to look closely at if we want to try and understand the complexity of pop and dance music in the 1980s. Throughout much of rock music history, critics have gravitated toward the great male genius as the epitome of rock's ability to communicate musically. For example, the Beatles and Bob Dylan are often talked about as the musicians who elevated the status of rock and roll. I love the Beatles and Dylan, but if we leave the dance music featured in this chapter out of the story, then we miss quite a lot about the history of rock and roll. Madonna's outrageous performances made critics and scholars stand up and take note of her sound, style, and message, and she continues to influence other musicians today.

SONG FACTS: "VOGUE" (1990)

Written by Madonna and Shep Pettibone | Released on Sire Records, March 1990

This song was released as part of the soundtrack to the film *Dick Tracy* (1990), which was based on a 1930s comic strip about a detective. The movie stars Madonna as a nightclub entertainer

opposite her (at the time) real-world boyfriend Warren Beatty. The concept of voguing was something Madonna picked up from a number of gay nightclubs around New York City. It is a dance in which the dancer uses facial expressions and hand gestures to pose like a famous movie star—as if taking a picture for the cover of Vogue magazine, hence the name. The lyrics of the song explain the idea and also name famous movie stars from the '20s until now. Madonna brought the dance to a worldwide audience, and the song continues to be one of Madonna's biggest international hits.

TRY THIS AT HOME

Sometimes dancing is just about moving your body to have a good time and feel the music. Other times it can be about communicating emotion or a story, and needs to be meticulously choreographed. While you might not be up to becoming the next rock tour choreographer, you can try to arrange a fun dance routine for your family or a group of your children's friends. See if you can come up with specific moves for each person. Are you all going to move together (Janet Jackson music video style) or is each person going to do his or her own thing? What do the moves mean? Are you going to try to relate to the lyrics or sound of the music? Have each person design their own routine using the same piece of music and see how different the end results are!

"VOGUE"

LISTENING GUIDE

Musically, this song is a fun combination of disco elements from the 1970s and the sound of house music from the 1980s. By listening to the arrangement and musical form of the song, we can hear how it was purposefully constructed for the dance floor—the first verse does not start until a minute and a half into the song. I am going to focus on that first minute and a half for the following Listening Guide.

0:00 | Instrumental Introduction The song opens with Madonna asking the listener, "What are you looking at," as a way to establish the visual nature of the song lyrics. The following synthesized string sounds work as a reference to both house music and the string sections of classic disco. The song then begins to build slowly with the addition of finger snaps, a pitched drum sound, and a deep pulsing bass (that one comes straight out of house music).

0:52 | Bring the Rhythm Not really a "new" section, but enough changes to point out the differences. The drum machine enters with a pattern that is very similar to the Chicago house music sound. Can you hear how the snare drum has a soft timbre? It doesn't pop like many other songs. If you relax and groove with the song, you can also hear how the drumbeat has a real ebb and flow to it, kind of like it wants you to sway with it. Listen to that snare. There is a digital sample of Madonna saying "Strike a pose" to explain the dance element of voguing. How do we know it is sampled? Her voice sounds clipped and a little bit like it does not belong in the space. Many songs in the late '80s and early '90s used a digital sampler to record small bits of dialogue from films or lyrics from other songs to add into the mix—a good example is M/A/R/R/S, "Pump Up the Volume" (1987). Here, Madonna just samples herself.

1:11 | Chorus Music If this is the first time you are hearing the song, then you wouldn't know it, but this is the music of the chorus section without the vocal melody. It's a great way to foreshadow the music.

1:26 | Verse 1 Madonna sings with a call and response style "echo" at the end of each line of the lyrics.

1:58 | Chorus Madonna sings the chorus hook while a synthesized piano plays typical house music chords, including minor 7ths and minor 9ths, in the background.

2:15 | Verse 2

2:48 | Chorus

3:05 | Bridge A new melody with a held out string/organ sound pulsing in the background. If you listen carefully, you can also hear that the bass is playing an octave higher than in the rest of the song.

3:27 | Chorus

3:44 | Break This part functions like the break of many disco songs; it's where the groove of the song really takes over.

4:00 | Rap Madonna raps out a sequence of famous movie stars.

4:34 | House Music Break The rap ends with another break. If the first one before the rap sounded like disco, then this one sounds like house music and focuses on the synthesized piano sound.

4:52 | Chorus

CHAPTER 6:

NEW ROCK SOUN

Stevie Nicks, 1977

Played: **FUNK/ROCK**

- PLAYLIST -

In the playlist below, songs recorded by Funkadelic are followed by an F, and Parliament by a P.

"Mommy, What's a Funkadelic?" (1970) F

"Cosmic Slop" (1973) F

"Up for the Down Stroke" (1974) P

"Give Up the Funk
(Tear the Roof off the Sucker)" (1976) P

"Dr. Funkenstein" (1976) P

"Mothership Connection (Star Child)" (1976) P

"Bop Gun (Endangered Species)" (1977) P

"Funkentelechy" (1978) P

"Flash Light" (1978) P

"One Nation Under a Groove" (1978) F

TRY THIS AT HOME

It's time to take the idea of the concept album to the next level—like, into outer space, baby! You're going to create a mythology for your own band. First, you need a story, so start thinking about an idea that might work for a musical journey. You might try to make the music the centerpiece of the story like P-Funk's idea of the "Funk." Who are your characters? If you want another example of how a band has used the mythology concept, then take a listen to the music of the rock band Coheed and Cambria. All of their albums are based on a single story called *The Amory Wars*.

Parliament-Funkadelic live circa 1982

In chapter 1, we heard how funk music began with James Brown merging soul and R&B to create a new form of dance music. But if we want to hear where funk music went after James, then we need to listen to the booty-shaking sounds of Parliament and Funkadelic. Many people don't realize that Parliament and Funkadelic were actually two separate bands that made different sonic versions of funk. Funkadelic was the first to release an album in 1970, playing funk that drew heavily from psychedelic rock. The sound of Parliament relied on a mixture of smooth R&B and dance music. Both bands featured the same sizeable cast of musicians, working with bandleader George Clinton (take a moment to go look it up online, the list is quite impressive). Clinton still tours with musicians who played with him during the 1970s, and they now use the name the P-Funk All Stars. So even though many people talk about the band Parliament–Funkadelic (as in the group of people), there was never an actual record recorded under that name.

HISTORICAL FACT/SOCIAL CONNECTIONS

Concept albums that feature multiple characters and elaborate stories are often seen as the purview of progressive rock—but the P-Funk Mythology takes it to a whole new level. The concepts, characters, and themes contained in this mythology played out across multiple albums and concert tours by both Parliament and Funkadelic. At its core is an idea presented in the first Funkadelic song, "Mommy, What's a Funkadelic?" In this song, we learn that the "Funk" is not from our world. It is from outer space and has come to Earth to bring good feelings. But we also learn that there are forces at work who want to stop the funk, like Sir Nose D'Voidoffunk (say it slow kids: Sir Nose Devoid of Funk), and others who fight for the funk, like the Starchild and Dr. Funkenstein, who came to Earth on the Mothership. Over the years, certain band members became known for their portrayal of these characters; for example Clinton was Dr. Funkenstein and Bootsy Collins was the Starchild (who played his fantastic star bass).

SONG FACTS: "FLASH LIGHT" (1978)

Written by George Clinton, Bootsy Collins, and Bernie Worrell

Released on Casablanca Records, January 1978

This song is based on a small number of musical ideas—but they sound so good, the song could just go on forever (and in some P-Funk shows it did). On the surface, the lyrics are pretty silly, and it all seems to be about a flashlight (Parliament did end up selling their own brand of flashlights at their concerts). But if you listen a little closer, you will hear the lyrics are about someone who says he will never dance. But other voices are saying that what he needs is the funk, "Shine the spotlight on him!" Although you would never know it from just listening to this one song, the lyrics tie into the larger P-Funk mythology. Sir Nose D'Voidoffunk is the person mentioned in the song who will not dance, and wants to put an end to the funk, mostly because he thinks he is too cool for it. But the hero of our song is Starchild, who uses the Bop Gun and his Flash Light to keep people dancing and ultimately defeats Sir Nose.

The Mothership descends as P-Funk performs on stage, June 4, 1977.

"FLASH LIGHT"

LISTENING GUIDE

Do you remember what I said was the most important thing about funk music (way back in chapter 1)? Groove—that rhythmic feeling in the music, a sense of swing as all the various musical elements come together. That feeling is very important in the music of Parliament. For the entire 10 minutes of the song, the various instruments play variations on their own short musical ideas (or motives), and it is only in the total coming together of these individual sounds that we can have the groove, the motion of the song. That's also why many people talk about funk music being a uniting force. As the musical sounds come together, it also represents a coming together of all the people under the Sun—one nation under the groove. Below you will find a list of some of the musical ideas—see if you can hear them in the song. When do they play? When do they stop? How do they relate to one another?

Bass | The bass line plays constantly throughout the entire song. While it was originally written by Bootsy for him to play on bass, the final song features Bernie Worrell playing the melody on the Moog synthesizer. Check out some of the cool synth effects he creates at the end of each major phrase.

Drums | The drums work as a constant pulse in the song—the foundation for the rest of the band to play around and against. The hand claps are prominent and work well on the dance floor to accent the backbeat.

Guitar | The clean electric guitar sound has just a little bit of reverb on it, and at times it features what is called a chorus effect—to make it sound like more than one guitar. It tends to play a single strummed rhythmic pattern with a number of variations. But listen carefully and you will hear how it switches to a picked melody in the mellow sections of the song.

Vocals | There is almost always a vocal melody or shout happening in the song, but sometimes there are so many people singing that it can be hard to hear exactly what is being said. Sometimes, the different vocal lines are all singing something different, what we call *polyphony*. This can be heard at moments like the one at the 3-minute mark when one group sings the line "help him find the funk," another sings "ha-da-dadee-da," and even more sing their own ad lib of the word "flashlight."

Synthesizers | There are several keyboard solos in the song, and most of them play in the upper register to distinguish the sound from the Moog bass in the low register.

QUEEN

Played: **GLAM ROCK/ROCK/ARENA ROCK**

‑ PLAYLIST ‑

"Killer Queen" (1974)

"Bohemian Rhapsody" (1975)

"Somebody to Love" (1976)

"We Will Rock You" (1977)

"We Are the Champions" (1977)

"Another One Bites the Dust" (1980)

"Crazy Little Thing Called Love" (1980)

"Under Pressure" [with David Bowie] (1982)

"Radio Ga Ga" (1984)

"I Want to Break Free" (1984)

"A Kind of Magic" (1986)

"The Show Must Go On" (1991)

Queen, 1976

Formed in London, England, in 1970, the band Queen became a worldwide sensation and fueled the rise of the arena rock style. Always looking for new musical inspiration, the band experimented in the early days by combining musical elements taken from diverse styles such as progressive rock, hard rock, heavy metal, disco, glam rock, gospel, folk, and even classical music and opera. It might be hard for you to imagine what all of that might sound like mixed together, but that was the point. Queen wanted to create something that was uniquely theirs, and had a strong emotional power at the center. The band consisted of Freddie Mercury (1946–1991) (vocals, piano), Brian May (guitar, vocals), John Deacon (bass), and Roger Taylor (drums). Mercury's voice was extremely powerful, and he had an extraordinary ability to control it precisely over a very wide range. Brian May's guitar solos have become the stuff of rock legend. Together, Mercury and May took the Plant and Page (Led Zeppelin) musical model into the next generation of rock.

Queen performs at Live Aid
(pictured, Mercury and May)

HISTORICAL FACT/SOCIAL CONNECTIONS

In 1984, Bob Geldof and Midge Ure had arranged for a group of mostly British musicians to record a song called "Do They Know It's Christmas?" under the name Band Aid as a way to raise awareness of the devastating Ethiopian famine. The crisis had gained worldwide attention at the time, and another star-studded charity song was soon made to benefit the same cause. "We Are the World" (1985) was recorded by USA for Africa and written by Michael Jackson and Lionel Richie. Based on the success of "Do They Know It's Christmas," Geldof and Ure wanted to do even more and created a global concert event to raise money. On July 13, 1985, they organized two concerts to take place in different locations at the same time: one at Wembley Stadium in London and the other at JFK Stadium in Philadelphia. Both shows contained a who's who list of mid-'80s performers, but one band stole the show: Queen. Their performance in London became the iconic performance of the entire event—one that many watched around the world on TV. The performance of "Radio Ga Ga" has often been voted as one of the best live performances of all time. Go watch it online right now and I guarantee you will be amazed by the band's energy and audience participation (particularly in the break of the song).

Written by Freddie Mercury

Released on EMI Records, November 1976

This song appeared on the self-produced 1976 Queen album *A Day at the Races*, which was a follow-up to their mega-successful 1975 album *A Night at the Opera* (both named after Marx Brothers movies). "Somebody to Love" was seen as a spiritual successor to the previous "Bohemian Rhapsody," in that it tried to create an over-the-top emotional roller coaster that featured complex vocal arrangements. While "Bohemian Rhapsody" took its vocal cue from opera, this song drew its inspiration from gospel.

Rock bands still use this kind of gospel vocal arrangement as in the 2013 hit song "Counting Stars" by One Republic (listen to the break at the 3-minute mark).

RY THIS AT HOME

It's time to break out the popcorn again and watch a rock and roll concert in our living room. As live performers, Queen really pushed at the boundaries of what was expected in live performance. Early on, they had adopted the use of costumes and staging common in glam rock, but once they began performing in large sold-out arenas, they began to think of the entire performance as a stage show: bigger lighting, more dramatic use of the space, and costumes. There are a number of Queen concerts available on DVD, so go pick one up and enjoy.

LISTENING GUIDE

"SOMBODY TO LOVE"

The musical sound of the song is the perfect way to express the emotion of the lyrics. The words present a man searching for love, fighting feelings of loneliness, and questioning his faith as he prays to God for help in finding true love. The elaborate vocal sounds make it appear as if a full choir is singing, but the entire arrangement was achieved by multitrack recording the band members singing different parts. Each part was recorded one at a time and built up like layers of a cake—an impressive accomplishment.

0:00 | Vocal Introduction This song begins with a soft piano chord to establish the musical key (as if it were a live performance) followed by the multilayered vocal parts singing the chorus of the song while the piano plays softly underneath. The piano then begins its own melody without the vocals to kick-start the full song.

0:27 | Verse 1 Mercury sings over the sounds of the drums, bass, guitar, and piano. The vocal choir from the introduction acts as a call and response to Mercury's voice (although lyrically they frequently anticipate his words).

0:47 | Chorus This section is an organic outgrowth of the verse, but the major difference is that the vocal choir moves to a supporting role as background singers.

1:03 | Verse 2

1:23 | Chorus This chorus adds a short tag (1:32–1:37) to transition the music into the bridge section.

1:38 | Bridge The rhythm shifts to a pounded ba-ba-ba, and even when Mercury and the vocals return to a melody that is closer to the verse, you can still hear the electric guitar and drums playing this rhythm in the background.

2:02 | Guitar Solo Brian May performs a solo on the electric guitar. Listen to the timbre of the guitar. It uses distortion, but overall the melody and tone are crisp and not too fuzzy.

2:23 | Chorus This time, the emotion of the ending tag material at 2:30 causes the choir to sing the chorus melody one more time—as if they can't contain themselves.

2:39 | Verse 3

3:00 | Break The band stops playing and the volume of the vocals drops to a soft whisper. They repeat the title of the song over and over as new voices join the chant. It starts in the low register but quickly begins to climb up and up as Mercury moans and sings in the background. The song builds up more and more as hand claps, drums, piano, yells, and shouts enter the mix.

3:42 | Chorus and Stop Once the buildup of the break is at its peak, the song enters the chorus—and then it stops abruptly. Mercury's voice makes one final solo plea to the heavens. Listen to how he does it. He starts with a high and loud shout, and as his voice uses a melisma to dive down to his lower register, it gets softer and softer.

3:58 | Chorus The song returns to the chorus melody and ideas, but now it repeats the short phrase of the song title. This works emotionally because the singer has now told his story and is totally focused on his plea, but it also works musically as a coda. The band and vocals drive home the main musical theme of the song. Don't miss the clipped piano chord at the end—once again creating the illusion that it is taken from a live performance.

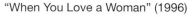
─ PLAYLIST ─

"Mystery Mountain" (1975)

"Lights" (1979)

"Wheel in the Sky" (1979)

"Any Way You Want It" (1980)

"Don't Stop Believin'" (1981)

"Who's Crying Now" (1981)

"Open Arms" (1981)

"Separate Ways (Worlds Apart)" (1983)

"Faithfully" (1983)

"Girl Can't Help It" (1986)

"When You Love a Woman" (1996)

Steve Perry and Neal Schon of Journey

Steve Perry

The band Journey had its beginnings in San Francisco in 1973, the result of guitarist Neal Schon and keyboardist Gregg Rolie looking to form a new band after they left the group Santana. In the beginning, their music had a jazz fusion sound (similar to some of Santana's music), and it transitioned into a progressive rock style by the time they recorded their first album *Journey* in 1975. While the music showcased the musicians' talents, it failed to resonate with a wider audience, and in 1977 they found singer Steve Perry to move the band in a more commercial direction. Between 1978 and 1981, they refined their sound, worked on their songwriting, and eventually released one of the biggest selling albums of the early 1980s, *Escape* (1981). This version of the band (with several new members) took note of Queen and created big melodic rock songs with strong vocal melodies. Journey was soon performing in sold out stadiums around the world.

HISTORICAL FACT/SOCIAL CONNECTIONS

In 1982, Journey was so popular that they even starred in their own video game for the Atari 2600 called *Journey Escape* (obviously based on the popularity of the album *Escape*). The concept of the game was to get the band members out of the stadium after a concert and through a gauntlet of wild fans and music industry types. While music-based games like Guitar Hero, Rock Band, Dance Dance Revolution, and Sing Star are commonplace today—and may even represent the main way some people buy music—they were unheard of in 1982. The game even featured an 8-bit version of "Don't Stop Believin'." Try to track it down, if you can, but be warned; as cool as the idea was, if I remember correctly the game was not very good.

Written by Jonathan Cain, Steve Perry, and Neal Schon

Released on Columbia Records, October 1981

This song was a major hit in 1981 (although it never reached number one on the *Billboard* charts), but what is truly amazing is that it continues to be one of the best-selling "back-catalog" songs ever (meaning it is an old song that you can still buy). A big part of this is because the emotional power of the song still resonates with listeners, and as a result it remains current. The song has been used in tons of movies to varying effect—as nostalgia, as camp, as over-the-top rock song, and as great music. It was also the first song recorded and released by the cast of the TV show *Glee* in 2009 (in the pilot episode), which caused a major revival for the music of Journey.

DESTINATIONS

This one's simple: go see a rock band play in a large stadium venue. Make a day of it and eat lunch in the parking lot tailgate style. For some of you that might mean somewhere close to home in your own city, but for others you might need to travel to a major city where a band is performing. There is something unique about listening and watching a band along with 40,000 other people. This is your chance to experience the sound and lights of a full rock arena performance as a family. I recommend bringing earplugs, especially for the younger ones, since the volume will most likely be very loud.

"DON'T STOP BELIEVIN'"

LISTENING GUIDE

In my opinion, this might just be the ultimate power ballad. The music is constructed in such a way as to toy with your anticipation and pull you into the rising emotion of the song. It has an unusual musical structure. It is all about the buildup and the increasing tension in the song, with the full chorus not even happening until the very end. By the time Perry sings "don't stop believing," you can't help but want to shout it out loud with him.

0:00 | Introduction Jonathan Cain's digital piano begins the song, and the chord progression it plays in the key of E major continues for almost the entire song: E major, B major, C Sharp minor, A major, E major, B major, G Sharp minor, and A major (I-V-vi-IV-I-V-iii-IV).

0:17 | Verse 1 Lyrically, this verse sets up the two major characters of the song: the small town girl and the city boy. Ross Valory's bass enters playing along with the left-hand part of the keyboard.

0:49 | Instrumental Section The electric guitar enters and builds to what sounds like the beginning of a solo and then stops as the song returns to the verse.

1:05 | Verse 2 Between the electric guitar leading into it and the drum fills leading out, this shortened verse has a sense of urgency to it.

1:20 | Prechorus/Bridge The move into this section feels like an important arrival. The instrumentation changes in a few important ways. The drums play for the first time, the keyboard switches to an electronic string sound, and the bass begins to play a number of melodic fills between the phrases. The guitar strums power chords in a steady rhythm with the drums. The chord progression that has been the basis of the entire song stops as the music just alternates between the A major and E major chords (IV and I). So what should we call this section? This is a good example of how thinking about song structure can involve careful thinking and a comparison of the various parts. This section feels like a chorus, but once we finally hear the last section of the song that seems like the chorus.

1:54 | Instrumental Section It might sound like we are headed to a full instrumental section or guitar solo, but it goes right back to the verse.

2:01 | Verse 3 The music really kicks into full gear here as drummer Steve Smith rocks it out and keeps the energy building.

2:33 | Prechorus/Bridge

3:05 | Instrumental Section Neal Schon finally takes the solo he has been threatening to play the entire time. Saving the solo for this late in the song works well with the lyrics; even when things seem their darkest, you need to believe in yourself and your dream. The solo finally playing feels like the musical realization of that ideal.

3:21 | Chorus Once the solo is over, Perry finally sings the main melody! This is the exact opposite of the song structure of Motown, where you heard the main hook first and then often, but like the solo it shows that determination can get you there. It uses the same chord progression as the verses, so one more time, it plays on the idea that the dream was there all along. This ending is much more effective than if the song went somewhere else musically to signify the arrival of the dream.

Played: **ROCK/HARD ROCK**

Heart in 1977 (clockwise from left: Roger Fisher, Howard Leese, Steve Fossen, Michael DeRosier, Nancy Wilson, and Ann Wilson)

The band that would become Heart started in the Seattle area of Washington in 1967 when Steve Fossen (bass) and Roger Fisher (guitar) formed the Army. The group played a mixture of hard rock and classic rock and roll. They really took off when sisters Ann and Nancy Wilson joined the group. Ann was a gifted songwriter and singer. She has often been called one of the best rock singers of all time for her ability to sing powerfully across a wide vocal range and to control her voice even when singing at a whisper. Her sister Nancy, also a songwriter, played guitar and sang.

I must say that I have never seen anybody rock an acoustic guitar quite like Nancy (seriously, go watch for yourself). During the late 1970s the band recorded a series of songs that have become mainstays of classic rock radio, such as "Magic Man" and "Barracuda." After a short hiatus in the early 1980s, the group reformed with a number of new members, and teamed with several hit-making songwriters like Bernie Taupin and Diane Warren. The result was another streak of popular songs including "Alone." The band continues to record, tour, and rock it out today.

Ann and Nancy Wilson perform live

Ann Wilson, 1977

HISTORICAL FACT/SOCIAL CONNECTIONS

The world has changed quite a bit over the last thirty years, and today women performers, songwriters, and producers have become a major part of the music industry. But when Heart started in the late 1970s, the world of rock—and particularly hard rock—was a boys' club in some of the worst ways. Ann and Nancy Wilson had to deal with this on several fronts. They had to fight on a daily basis to be considered serious musicians (which they are) and not just as sex objects used to sell records (see the story of "Barracuda" if you need an example). Stereotypes regarding talent and sexuality/gender are still present today. What images do you see representing women in the music industry today? How do women continue to break down gender stereotypes? Take a listen to Kacey Musgraves' "Follow Your Arrow" (2013), a humorous song that talks about many of the gender and social issues women still face.

Written by Ann Wilson, Nancy Wilson, Michael DeRosier, and Roger Fisher

Released on Portrait Records, May 1977

This rocking song was the first single from the 1977 album *Little Queen*. Ann tells it, she wrote the song as a response to the publicity stunt that their label Mushroom Records tried, basically telling people that Ann and Nancy were lesbian lovers in some strange attempt to entice male audiences to buy more records. An odd tactic in the first place made even stranger by the fact that they were sisters). The barracuda of the song's lyrics is Ann's depiction of the record industry executives as backstabbing sharks in the water. One verse even features the direct line "no right, no wrong, selling a song" as her version of the label's response to the situation.

ESTINATIONS

Take a trip to the home of Heart, the city of Seattle, Washington. The city has always been a home to great rock and roll music. There are still a lot of great live music venues to check out, some good food and coffee, and you can even visit the Experience Music Project Museum (EMP). The EMP started as a music museum then it was launched by Microsoft co-founder Paul Allen in 2000, but since then they have added exhibits about popular culture and it is now home to the Science Fiction Museum and Hall of Fame. So if you're into rock and roll and science fiction, this trip is the perfect double shot of espresso for you!

"BARRACUDA"

LISTENING GUIDE

Oh, by the way, did I mention that this song seriously rocks! The galloping rhythm setup at the very start pervades the entire song with a constant sense of movement. Ann's voice jumps quickly from the highest heights, pushing out a rising melodic line, down to a quiet turn of phrase that bites with the best kind of intimacy. Fisher's guitar solo features a great melody that hangs up in certain sections and then blazes forward in others, while the bass and drums played by Fossen and Michael DeRosier keep the beat driving the entire time.

0:00 | Introduction The guitar opens the song with the signature galloping riff that features a cool use of the whammy bar at the end of the phrase. When the riff repeats the bass guitar joins in playing the same rhythm and melody. The third time the drums enter playing a 4/4 rhythm with a backbeat. The riff repeats one more time to make a nice even four.

0:28 | Verse 1 Ann's voice enters and soars above the instruments. Listen to how her melody is shaped. It rises up to a high note that she holds out, and then moves down to a lower note at the end of each phrase.

0:51 | Chorus This section does not feel like an abrupt break from the verse, as the rhythm continues to push forward. But you will notice that Ann sings a new melody and the band responds by playing a new chord progression. The music makes a dramatic stop at the end of the chorus so that we simply hear Ann saying the hook, "well wouldn't cha, Barracuda."

1:05 | Instrumental Break
1:19 | Verse 2

1:41 | Chorus 2 Since this song is telling a continuous story as Ann sings, you will notice that the lyrics of the chorus are not a direct repetition of the first chorus (as they often are in rock and roll).

1:55 | Instrumental Break

2:02 | Bridge This section features several ideas. It begins with a new melody sung by Ann and a descending melody from the band. Then the main guitar riff returns and pulls the song back to the verse music. Ann repeats the new melody, which once again ends with the guitar returning to the main riff.

2:29 | Instrumental Bridge/Guitar Solo 1 A fun but short guitar solo. If you listen carefully you will hear how it uses Ann's new melody from the bridge section—and that, in fact, this whole section is actually an instrumental version of the bridge. Listen for the forceful acoustic guitar strumming in the background.

2:56 | Chorus 3

3:16 | Guitar Solo 2 This is an extended guitar solo that builds over the course of a full minute. It starts with single notes and strummed chords bent with the whammy bar. Listen to how the drums and bass play less aggressively to create a nice space for the guitar to play in. A new sound enters that sounds like a mix between a synthesizer and an electric guitar, making what I think is best described as "shooting star" sounds. Listen for it. What name would you give it?

4:05 | Truncated Riff to End The song ends with a shortened variation on the main guitar, bass, and drum riffs.

FLEETWOOD MAC

Played: **BLUES ROCK / SOFT ROCK / POP ROCK**

~ PLAYLIST ~

"Albatross" (1968)

"Spare Me a Little of Your Love" (1972)

"Rhiannon" (1975)

"Landslide" (1975)

"Don't Stop" (1977)

"Go Your Own Way" (1977)

"Tusk" (1979)

"Gypsy" (1982)

"Hold Me" (1982)

"Big Love" (1987)

"Little Lies" (1987)

"Save Me" (1990)

"Peacekeeper" (2003)

Fleetwood Mac circa 1975 (l to r: John McVie, Lindsey Buckingham, Christine McVie, Stevie Nicks, and Mick Fleetwood).

The story of Fleetwood Mac is really a story about two different bands. The group was originally formed in 1967 by Peter Green in London as part of the British blues revival movement. The group was named after two of Green's friends who played blues with him, drummer Mick Fleetwood and bassist John McVie (known as Mac), and who have been the rhythm section of Fleetwood Mac for most of its long existence. The major shift happened in 1975 when Fleetwood, McVie, and his wife Christine (who joined the band as singer/songwriter and keyboard player) were looking for some new musicians to join the group after the departure of many of the original members. The result was the second and more famous lineup that still exists today, including two American musicians, guitarist/singer Lindsey Buckingham and singer Stevie Nicks. They created a new soft rock sound for the 1970s, and their 1977 album *Rumours* is one of the all-time great records.

evie Nicks performs in Cleveland,
hio, 1977

ritten by Stevie Nicks

eleased on Reprise Records, 1975

his was one of the initial songs
at singer Stevie Nicks brought to
eetwood Mac as a songwriter. Nicks
d Buckingham had been performing
a duo before they joined Fleetwood
ac, but their first and only studio album
uckingham Nicks was a commercial
lure. That disappointment was hard for
cks to take, and she ended up writing
is song as a way to deal with what she
t was a landslide in her life: falling from
e heights of making a record. But as
any songwriters do, she was able to
oaden the meaning of the lyrics and
e result was a haunting song about lost
ve, change, and about trying to stay
ounded. As a result many listeners are
le to find connections to their own life
the words of the song.

"LANDSLIDE"

Musically, "Landslide" is a beautiful and subtle song that features the impressive finger-picking of guitarist Lindsey Buckingham. As you listen to the song, pay close attention to the timbre of Nicks's voice. Her voice sits in the contralto range, which allows her to have a deep resonance in some moments. She sings the smooth, rolling melody of "Landslide" in legato tones that evoke a feeling of calm. But underneath all that, there is a rough growl in her voice. Nicks has cited Janis Joplin and Grace Slick as her musical influences, and both of those women also performed with a little bit of grit in their voices. In this song, that element of Nicks's voice allows for a perceived sense of intimacy in the music. As listeners, we can close our eyes and it almost feels like she is sitting next to us, singing the song as we look out on the mountains in the distance.

0:00 | Guitar Introduction The entire opening is played on acoustic guitar. If you pay attention, you can hear the result of Buckingham's picking style. Try to follow just one series of notes for a moment. For example, focus on the low bass notes he is playing. Notice that they make a four-note pattern: D sharp, down to D, down to C, and back up to D. A different pattern is made by the higher notes to create the main guitar melody.

0:12 | Verse 1 Nicks's voice enters softly as she sings the first verse of the song. Can you hear how she uses vibrato on the longer notes toward the end of the verse? The title of the song appears at the end of this verse.

0:35 | Verse 2 Nicks's continues into the second verse, but pay attention to how she increases the volume of her voice this time and sings more of the melody in her upper register. There is a short extension of the music here and we can hear Nicks humming over it.

1:12 | Bridge This section features a new picking pattern in the guitar and a new melody for the vocal.

1:37 | Guitar Solo Buckingham's solo is full of restrained beauty. It frequently holds up on notes, much like the emotions that Nicks sings about. At the end of the solo, Buckingham performs a musical landslide, of sorts, as he plays his first fast melodic run down to a low note.

2:00 | Bridge The electric guitar from the solo plays in the background as a call and response to Nicks's voice. If you look at the overall form of this song, you will see that it is a bit like a palindrome, although the rise and fall of the music often distracts us from that fact: verse, verse, bridge, solo, bridge, verse, and (verse).

2:32 | Verse 3 Even though this song is mellow, you will notice that the energy level of the guitar and Nicks's voice drop even more on her line, "take my love and take it down." But don't worry; the song is not over just yet. The music pulls us back in as the volume increases at the 2:55 mark.

At the 3-minute mark there is a short but cool break. I think it is interesting because it is so unexpected. The music of the final verse had just started to build up and then, all of a sudden, it stops. Emotionally, it is a great effect, possibly alluding to the unexpected things in life. The vocals and guitar begin again and play softly to the end.

HALL & OATES

Played: **SOFT ROCK/SOUL/POP ROCK**

⌐ PLAYLIST ⌐

"She's Gone" (1974)

"Sara Smile" (1976)

"Rich Girl" (1977)

"Kiss on My List" (1981)

"Private Eyes" (1981)

"I Can't Go for That (No Can Do)" (1981)

"Maneater" (1982)

"One on One" (1983)

"Out of Touch" (1984)

"Method of Modern Love" (1985)

"Everything Your Heart Desires" (1988)

"So Close" (1990)

Hall & Oates (l to r: John Oates and Daryl Hall), 1979

Daryl Hall and John Oates were both playing in bands in their native Philadelphia when they met in 1967. They shared a love for folk and soul music—particularly the sounds of Motown and Philly Soul. Their first album for Atlantic Records in 1972 called Whole Oats was produced by the legendary Arif Mardin, but the soft rock sound failed to gain an audience. For their second album the duo tried to add more soul sounds to the mix with songs like "She's Gone." It worked, and they eventually went on to be one of the most successful recording duos of all time. Their early-'80s records like Private Eyes and H2O helped to define the sound of the entire era. Their big polished sound fell out of vogue in the 1990s, but they have recently seen a resurgence in popularity, mostly due to the enduring nature of their songwriting. Now Daryl Hall can be seen performing on his television show *Live at Daryl's House* where he frequently plays classic Hall and Oates songs with current artists.

Hall & Oates live in 1983

HISTORICAL FACT/SOCIAL CONNECTIONS

The name blue-eyed soul was often used to describe bands like Hall & Oates who played a variation of soul music. The term originally developed in the early 1960s, when issues of segregation were still prominent in the United States. Remember that some black musicians like Chuck Berry couldn't even perform in clubs in the 1950s because of intense racial discrimination. The term blue-eyed soul was used to describe white performers who played music inspired by Motown and Stax. One early example was the Righteous Brothers' 1964 album called Some *Blue Eyed Soul*. Many artists did not like the term because it continued to imply a racial division of the music, meaning soul music was only made by black performers and blue-eyed soul by white ones. However, once the term caught on it stuck and was used throughout much of the 1970s and 1980s.

ll & Oates live in 1982

ritten by Daryl Hall and John Oates

eleased on Atlantic Records, 1974

hen this song was first released in 74, it did not do very well on the arts, but once Hall & Oates became opular two years later, the song was eleased and has since become a key ng in their repertoire. It was produced Arif Mardin, who was well known for ability as an arranger, and as a result e sound of this song is lush and evolves er the 5-minute running time.

ESTINATIONS

t on the road and head out to visit other musical city and experience some that classic Philly soul (and hopefully me cheesesteaks as well). Philly Soul sic featured such artists as the O'Jays, rold Melvin & the Blue Notes, and ddy Pendergrass, so make sure to d up your music devices with the right sic for the road trip. While you're there, ke sure to check out the place where se great artists recorded their music at ladelphia International Records.

"SHE'S GONE"

LISTENING GUIDE

I mentioned that Hall & Oates were one of the great rock and roll songwriting teams, and I think a big reason for that is how their lyrics and melodies work so well together. Sometimes, when you are singing a song, it can feel like the words are being forced into a melodic shape or that the melody is making a turn only to accommodate the words. In the case of Hall & Oates, it always feels like the two were conceived of as one single unit (even if the actual writing process would suggest otherwise). Listen to how lines in this love song like "sorry Charlie for the imposition" just flow out (and how that line could be really stilted if not handled the right way). The words also tell a great story that you can picture in your mind's eye, like the line "I'd pay the devil to replace her" as the singer feels the regret of letting his loved one go.

0:00 | Instrumental Introduction The opening of the song is dominated by the drums and the digital piano. Listen to how the ticking of the hi-hat cymbal marks out the time as the digital piano plays a syncopated series of chords. Just before the 30-second mark, strings begin to crescendo in the background and the electric guitar plays a short melody that stalls out. At 50 seconds, Hall and Oates sing "ohhhhh" in harmony and the song finally begins the first verse as a synthesizer tone rises up.

1:02 | Verse 1 The mellow groove from the opening continues with the drums playing a fuller backbeat pattern and a synthesizer tone holding a low drone. Listen for the wah-wah guitar playing soft chords in the background. I love how both Hall and Oates sing the song at the same time in the verse, one singing in the low register and one in the high.

1:27 | Verse 2 The synthesizer and the strings begin to assert themselves more in the mix. The voices finally swell along with them to transition the song to the first chorus.

1:52 | Chorus Almost 2 minutes have gone by and we have the first chorus. Listen to how full the arrangement sounds at this point when you compare it to the opening. We can now hear the full string section, drums, bass, and guitar,

and then the synthesizer playing behind the multiple vocal lines singing in harmony.

2:12 | Verse 3
2:36 | Chorus

2:55 | Saxophone Solo A great saxophone solo played over the music of the verse that finally ends on a high point and then lets the bottom drop out to go back to a soft quiet verse.

3:29 | Verse I love the sounds made by the string section in this verse.

3:53 | Chorus

4:10 | Buildup After the end of the chorus, the band begins to play a pulsing rhythm. When the new horn section enters, the song does something really interesting; it begins a series of key modulations and finally ends up in a higher key for the last chorus. This was a common musical trick in '70s music, but it is handled masterfully here.

4:36 | Chorus The music repeats and fades out to the end as Hall and Oates repeat "she's gone" over and over.

BRUCE SPRINGSTEEN

Played: **ROCK / SINGER-SONGWRITER**

⌐ PLAYLIST ⌐

"Blinded by the Light" (1973)

"Born to Run" (1975)

"The Promised Land" (1978)

"Hungry Heart" (1980)

"The River" (1981)

"Dancing in the Dark" (1984)

"Born in the USA" (1984)

"Tunnel of Love" (1987)

"Streets of Philadelphia" (1994)

"The Rising" (2002)

"We Take Care of Our Own" (2012)

Born in Long Branch, New Jersey, Springsteen got hi start playing in a series of bands on the Jersey Shore places like Asbury Park. He signed a recording contra with Columbia Records in 1972 and has been a majo force in popular music since. He frequently performs with his band called the E Street Band that consists of top-notch musicians, and is known for performing concerts that last for several hours. Springsteen is a great example of the singer-songwriter style that developed in the 1970s. His songs often tell stories of everyday people, something that connects him to the long tradition of folk music and musicians like Bot Dylan. Musically, he borrows liberally from the history of rock and roll using ideas that range from the girl groups of the 1960s to gospel music and the sounds of New York City punk rock. All of this is contained within a public persona that speaks of authenticity—when "the boss" speaks, yo believe what he is saying comes from the heart.

DESTINATIONS

The Jersey Shore has long been a destination in the summertime for families looking to have some fun on vacation. Unfortunately, in the last several years, the area has suffered an image problem (the many drunken escapades shown on the *Jersey Shore* television show may discourage some folks from visiting) and another more serious problem in the form of the devastation hurled at it by Hurricane Sandy. Small towns along the shore feature hotels, shops, restaurants, and music venues. So take a trip by the sea and help bring these once vibrant communities back to life. Sometimes, you can still catch Bruce playing there with his band!

HISTORICAL FACT/SOCIAL CONNECTIONS

Clarence Clemons, Bruce Springsteen, and Nils Lofgren perform in 1984

The singer-songwriter movement that developed in the 1970s was nothing new; simply that a sing musician would write and perform his/her own music. Musicians like James Taylor and Carole King began to sing songs about their own life, usually accompanied by sparse instrumentation; they projected a sense of truth and realness that audiences were looking for. After the artifice of late 1960s rock, the singer-songwriters suggeste a return to the ideals of the acoustic folk music aesthetic and it felt more honest to audiences. The entire idea was a revival of a concept from the Romantic era of the nineteenth century, one that projected musicians and artists as tortured individuals who poured their heart out onto the page while sitting at home on a rainy day (think of Beethoven or Van Gogh). This was quite different from the way many pop songs had been written up to that time—with a strict division of labor between those who wrote the music, those who wrot the lyrics, and those who performed.

ritten by Bruce Springsteen

eleased on Columbia Records, 1975

his is the first song on side two of the bum *Born to Run* from 1975. This was pringsteen's third album for Columbia d in many ways it was his attempt to hieve mainstream success. While the usic aims to sound like a classic rock d roll tune, the lyrics present a timeless ck and roll story of fast cars, a little wn that can't hold its protagonist, a l named Wendy, and a knowledge that ey were born to run. The story is semi-itobiographical and thus the realness of e events can be heard in Springsteen's ice. By listening to the album, we can ar that Springsteen not only tried to ake a record that sounded better than s first two, he also turned out some cellent songwriting with tunes like enth Avenue Freeze-Out" and the title ck "Born to Run."

LISTENING GUIDE

"BORN TO RUN"

With this epic song, Springsteen was trying to capture the fullness and excitement of the Phil Spector–produced girl group records of the '60s and the famous sound called the "wall of sound." *Born to Run* contains many different musical layers, but it also works well as a unified whole; nothing sounds out of place in the full-tilt musical momentum of the song.

0:00 | Instrumental Introduction A short rapid-fire drum fill from drummer Ernest "Boom" Carter breaks the silence and then the entire band enters the space that is awash in reverb. The space sounds big and activated. Listen to all the instruments playing including saxophone, several guitars, drums, bass, keyboards, and even chimes. The main musical theme is played in the electric guitar and chimes.

0:15 | Verse 1 (part 1) In this guide, I have broken each verse down into three separate sections. I think you can easily hear all three as a single unit, but I want you to listen for the ways that each section is different. In this first part of verse 1, you can hear that the band has laid back from the energy of the opening instrumental. The main instruments here are drums, bass, and acoustic guitar. This leaves more room for Springsteen to sing the first two lyrical phrases and establish the story without having to compete with the band.

0:28 | Verse 1 (part 2) In the second section, the bass begins to play a more melodic line and the chimes enter as Springsteen pushes his voice into a more aggressive space. It also sounds like it cuts out early as he sings "Ohhhh." If you count the measures, it turns out it is shortened. The intro and part one were both eight measures long and this is only six. What effect does that have on you as a listener?

0:39 | Verse 1 (part 3) The music has now built up to a level that is almost equal to the density of the opening. The end of this eight-measure part features the refrain "born to run."

0:51 | Instrumental Break Repeats the melodic theme from the opening with the full band playing.

1:03 | Verse 2 (part 1) The structure of verse 1 repeats here with this part of verse 2 using the mellow sound. One change is that the organ is featured in the second four measures.

1:16 | Verse 2 (part 2)
1:26 | Verse 2 (part 3)
1:40 | Instrumental Break

1:52 | Saxophone Solo A fantastic saxophone solo from Springsteen's longtime friend and fellow musician Clarence Clemons.

2:12 | Bridge So far, the entire song has been a series of short buildups in the instrumentation and the song now breaks into an entirely different feel for this bridge. The lyrics also take on a dreamlike aspect. At the end of the section (2:39), the band pushes the music back into the reality of the rest of the song. Listen closely for the several rhythmic variations of the main melodic line—several electric guitars, chimes, piano, and saxophone.

3:06 | Verse 3 (part 1)
3:18 | Verse 3 (part 2)
3:29 | Verse 3 (part 3)

The final verse features an extended ending that allows Springsteen to repeat the hook "born to run" several times.

3:55 | Instrumental and Vocal Coda

KISS

Played: HARD ROCK / GLAM ROCK / HEAVY METAL

Gene Simmons and Peter Criss (behind drums) of Kiss, 1978

Kiss had its roots in a New York City–based band called Wicked Lester that was founded by Gene Simmons (bass, vocals) and Paul Stanley (vocals, rhythm guitar) and played a late '60s–inspired form of hard rock. Paul and Gene decided that they wanted the band to begin staging more elaborate shows in the manner of Alice Cooper, and in 1973 they formed a new band with Peter Criss (drums, vocals) and Ace Frehley (guitar) and thus the original version of Kiss was born.

While their early music is straight-ahead hard rock in songs like "Black Diamond," their stage shows and appearance became something quite imaginative and saw them dressed in black, white, and silver costumes and wearing face paint. Each band member adopted a comic book–like character: the Starchild (Paul), the Demon (Gene), the Spaceman (Ace), and the Cat (Peter). The characters began to appear in the album artwork and the band's many, many merchandise offerings. Over the years Kiss has undergone a number of lineup changes—both with and without the makeup.

HISTORICAL FACT/SOCIAL CONNECTIONS

Rock and roll has grown up side by side with twentieth-century commercialism and the idea of merchandise. When Elvis Presley performed in the late 1950s, the various venues sold wallets, key chains, and pins with his image on it. There can be no doubt that his movies helped to sell music and vice versa. When Beatlemania hit in 1964, everything from lunchboxes to earrings had the Fab Four's faces on it, and it was even possible to buy a wig to get the Beatles haircut. Very early in their career, Kiss decided that they were going to license their image for all kinds of products. This included an official Marvel comic book, action figures, a pinball game, trading cards, an official Kiss record player, a toy guitar, and much, much more (including a movie—which we will never speak about again—it's not good, folks). Many people criticized the band in the late 1970s for selling out and making it more about the product than the music, but today the trend has only increased with artists offering merchandising for kids and adults alike.

ce Frehley, 1978

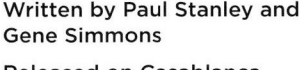

Written by Paul Stanley and Gene Simmons

Released on Casablanca Records, 1975

The original version of this song appears on the band's 1975 album *Dressed to Kill* and the song was even released as a single later that year, both of which were quickly eclipsed by a live recording of the song from the bum *Alive!* from later that year. This makes perfect sense since Gene nd Paul originally wrote the song with their live concerts in mind. They anted a song that had a great sing-along chorus that would work ell at the end of their shows, and they came up with the chant "I want rock and roll all night and party every day."

RY THIS AT HOME

aul Stanley, 1977

When performing live some bands try to reproduce the sound of the record as accurately as they can, so that the audience recognizes all the parts and can sing along and enjoy it. Other bands take the live performance as an opportunity to change ome songs or even use a particular song as a chance to improvise. 'e just heard the live version of "Rock and roll All Nite" by KISS from eir famous live album *Alive!*. Now take a listen to the original studio cording. What do you hear that is different? How have they changed e song? Which one do you like better? Why? Now go and compare e live and studio versions of some other songs you like. What fferences can you hear? What stays the same?

"ROCK AND ROLL ALL NITE"

LISTENING GUIDE

This listening guide uses the live version of the song—especially since that's pretty much the only one you will hear played on the radio anymore.

0:00 | Spoken Introduction The song opens with lead singer Paul Stanley addressing the crowd, thanking them for being a "dynamite" audience. When you listen to this within the context of the *Alive!* album, it's a great moment that gives you the sense that you are really there in the crowd.

0:27 | Instrumental Introduction The music begins with Peter Criss playing the signature drumbeat of the song in 4/4 time. It features the kick drum playing on beats 1 and 3 and the snare playing the typical backbeat on two and four. What makes it so identifiable is the tom-tom drums playing eighth notes throughout the introduction. The toms are what give it the boom-boom-bah feeling. The guitar and bass then enter playing the basic riff of the song.

0:41 | Verse 1 Gene Simmons sings the verses that feature lyrics enticing the listeners to join the party. The verse ends with a musical break after the lyrics "you keep on shouting" in which the bass and guitar stop playing and the drums play over the audience sounds and clapping. This serves as a great moment to build energy before the chorus.

1:14 | Chorus The full band starts playing again on the singalong chorus. At the end of the chorus, the bass and guitar stop again. Gene and Paul sing the chorus hook over Peter Criss's drumming—now heavy on the cymbals.

1:42 | Verse 2 The song's opening riff brings us back to the verse, which again ends with the guitar and bass break.

2:18 | Chorus

2:50 | Guitar Solo The original version of the song does not feature a solo, but in the live version, Ace gets a moment to shine and pump up the audience with a blues-style solo over the music of the verse. It ends like all the verses with the break into the chorus.

3:23 | Chorus This final chorus features the same guitar and bass break, but now the background sounds are mixed much louder, and we get the sense that the audience is going wild and clapping along.

Debbie Harry, 1979

CHAPTER 1:

NEW WAVE →

ROXY MUSIC

Played: **ART ROCK/GLAM ROCK/ROCK/DANCE/ELECTRONIC**

⟶ PLAYLIST ⟵

"Re-Make/Re-Model" (1972)

"Ladytron" (1972)

"Do the Strand" (1973)

"All I Want Is You" (1974)

"Love Is the Drug" (1975)

"Angel Eyes" (1979)

"Dance Away" (1979)

"Over You" (1980)

"More Than This" (1982)

"Avalon" (1982)

"The Main Thing" (1982)

Bryan Ferry, 1975

Roxy Music wanted to embody the essence of pop music and, at the same time, push at its limits by enacting a sense of musical experimentation. The core members of the group included Bryan Ferry (vocals), Phil Manzanera (guitar), Andy Mackay (saxophone), and Paul Thompson (drums), but over the years, the group also featured several additional musicians including Brian Eno (who played synthesizer in the early days), Eddie Jobson, and John Wetton. One of the most interesting aspects of Roxy Music was the way they purposefully drew upon musical ideas from many sources Elvis, the Beatles, the Rolling Stones, Pink Floyd, the Velvet Underground, and even King Crimson. They wanted their music to feel slick and modern with a bit of an avant-garde edge to it—and I think it still has that modern feeling today.

Roxy Music, circa 1975 [l to r: (back) Paul Thompson, Eddie Jobson, Phil Manzanera; (front) Andy Mackay, Bryan Ferry, and John Wetton]

HISTORICAL FACT/SOCIAL CONNECTIONS

Many British bands during the 1970s featured members who attended art school, including three of Roxy Music's members (Ferry, Mackay, and Eno). Students studied the visual arts and were part of a creative environment that often fostered an interest in music and literature. These schools produced a large number of musicians who were excited about finding ways to mix music with fashion, graphic design (think about the cool album covers of the era), theater, and literature. These musicians were predisposed to the avant-garde, having learned about it in school, and they wanted to bring it into their pop music. For example, listen to "Ladytron," from the first Roxy Music album. It moves through several different sections including experimental electronics, a pop song, psychedelic rock, and even a short "freak out" section at the end.

SONG FACTS: "LOVE IS THE DRUG" (1975)

Written by Bryan Ferry and Andy Mackay

Released on Atco Records, 1975

This song comes from the 1975 Roxy Music album *Siren* and continues to be their most popular song. The song produces a fantastic musical mood that describes the feeling of love as an addiction. If you watch their 1975 performance of the song on the television show *Supersonic*, you can see how they used fashion and presentation in their live performances. Ferry and the background singers are dressed in World War II–era military clothes while the rest of the band wears mid-'70s hipster fashion.

TRY THIS AT HOME

Look around in your community and see if you can find an art class that everyone in your family can take. If you live in a big city look for an art museum or an art school. If you live in a more rural area, try looking for a local college or public library. You might even try looking for a local art studio or pottery shop that offers classes. Your visual arts lessons might even inspire new ideas for music, just as they did for the members of Roxy Music. Can you find ways to connect the two? What about making some artwork inspired by music (after all, it worked for Jackson Pollock and Andy Warhol).

"LOVE IS THE DRUG"

LISTENING GUIDE

This song is a good example of how Roxy Music used the skeleton of pop song structure (it has the feeling of a verse–chorus song), but the actual sections never quite behave the way the formula wants them to. Be sure to listen to the interesting use of percussion and saxophone throughout. This song is fun to listen to loud, but listen on headphones to hear the depth of the performance.

0:00 | Introduction The song opens with the sound of shoes walking on stones. If you listen closely, it sounds like the ground is wet as the person makes their way over to a car and opens the door. A sharp guitar chord activates the band. The bass begins to play, pulsing on a single low note. A saxophone plays two lonely notes as we hear the engine of the car start, and pull away.

0:22 | Instrumental Introduction Cool sound on the digital piano. The introduction of the clarion call in the saxophone. The D minor to A minor chord progression established here serves as the basis for most of the song.

0:52 | Vocal Introduction You may think that this part sounds like a chorus the first time you hear the song, but these words never come back and the vocal melody sung here by Ferry is approximated in the only actual chorus later on.

1:07 | Verse 1 The verse keeps the musical groove from the opening going as Ferry sings about how he is out on the town looking to find love. He uses evocative lines to paint that picture, including one of my favorites that depicts a dance club, "Boy meets girl where the beat goes on." Listen to the way that Ferry sings the song. His voice has a deep and fluid tone to it, but what is really interesting is how he sometimes stammers out the words. The first word he sings in the verse is "aggravated." But when you hear him sing, it's like "Agg-ro . . . va . . . TED."

1:39 | Chorus The music stays almost the same as the verses but with a little bit more of the organ playing. The new chorus melody contains four phrases. The first and the third start with a held out "oh" from Ferry and the second and third start with the words "love is the drug."

1:54 | Postchorus If the verse is about the singer looking for love in various nightclubs, and the chorus is about his need to find love, then the postchorus sections are where he finally finds love—as fleeting as it might be. Ferry again sings "oh," but listen to how different it is from the one at the start of the chorus. Musically, the band represents the emotional response to love the biggest harmonic changes we have heard so far. It's a moment that breaks the monotony of the simple two-chord oscillation of verse and chorus. The instrumental melody that plays in response to Ferry's "oh" will later show up as the final vocal melody that closes the song.

2:10 | Verse 2

2:41 | Chorus

2:56 | Chorus (repeated)

3:12 | Chorus-Style Verse This double chorus uses little bits of music from different parts of the song up to this point. The "oh, ohs" are a variation of the "oh" from the first line of the chorus. The clarion sax sounds are from the opening instrumental introduction, and the musical backing and melodic phrasing comes from the verses.

3:42 | Postchorus One last ecstatic Postchorus takes us to the close of the song.

BLONDIE

Played: **PUNK/NEW WAVE/DANCE**

⊶ PLAYLIST ⊷

"In the Flesh" (1977)

"Denis" (1978)

"One Way or Another" (1978)

"Heart of Glass" (1978)

"Atomic" (1980)

"Call Me" (1980)

"The Tide Is High" (1980)

"Rapture" (1980)

"War Child" (1982)

"Maria" (1999)

"Good Boys" (2003)

"Rapture Riders" (2005)

Debbie Harry, 1978

Blondie perform during the Parallel Lines tour, 1978

Blondie is a great example of how a musical group can't always be defined within a single musical style. The band formed in New York City in 1975 and started playing in punk clubs like Max's Kansas City and CBGB. The lineup consisted of Debbie Harry (vocals), Chris Stein (guitar), Clem Burke (drums), Gary Valentine (bass), and Jimmy Destri (keyboards). Their early music has the energy of punk rock, but the instrumentation (featuring prominent use of organ) and the vocal melodies sung by Harry connect it to early 1960s girl group music; just listen to "In the Flesh." In 1978, they released what I consider to be one of the best albums of the late 1970s, *Parallel Lines*. The record features songs like "One Way or Another" that show the band finding a unique musical home somewhere between punk rock and traditional rock and roll. Much like Roxy Music, they were creating a modern sound by using elements of the past, an aspect that became a major part of new wave music. Blondie broke up in the early 1980s, but they continue to re-form from time to time to record new music and go out on tour.

HISTORICAL FACT/SOCIAL CONNECTIONS

The music of Blondie gives us a fascinating view into the various sounds of New York City during the late 1970s. In the live music clubs downtown, the sounds of punk rock were still creating a stir as the music slowly morphed into the more diverse post punk and new wave. The mixture of Cuban and Puerto Rican sounds saw the rise of salsa music in the Latin community. In uptown Manhattan, dance floors in nightclubs like Studio 54 were packed with people dancing to the newest disco sounds. And in the Bronx, the sounds of DJs (disc jockeys) and MCs (masters of ceremonies) performing at block parties were helping to form the basis of hip hop. A musician at the time could travel to clubs and parties around the city and hear all of these sounds, and in the case of Blondie, they tried to mix these elements together, pushing the development of new sounds ahead even further.

Debbie Harry of Blondie

ONG FACTS: "RAPTURE"

980)

ritten by Deborah Harry and
hris Stein

eleased on Chrysalis Records,
ovember 1980

his song is a perfect mix of disco and
&B sounds, as performed through the
rsonality of new wave, and it even
atures a hip hop–inspired rap at the
d—hence the title. Because hip hop
arted in the Bronx as a live music
dition and did not find its way onto
ecord until 1979, it allowed for the
velopment of a strange historical fact:
is song actually hit the mainstream
op market before the hip hop music
at inspired it. For the lyrics Harry
me up with her own surrealistic story
out life in New York City that seems
fit right in with the rest of Blondie's
usic, but she also added in several
tchphrases that were popular within
a hip hop community at the time such
"and you don't hip hop," and "you don't
op, sure shot." There is even a cool
t where she changes the end of that
t lyric to say "and you don't stop, do
nk rock."—a call back to Blondie's own
ginnings.

RY THIS AT HOME

ke some inspiration from the music of
ndie and the hip hop of New York City
d go make your own musical mashup.
e idea of a musical mashup has existed
ne form or another since the beginning
time—taking two types of music and
xing them together. Download some
sic mashup software to your computer,
let, or phone and try it for yourself.

"RAPTURE"

The music settles into a groove early on and stays with it for most of the song. But listen closely. Can you hear all the subtle variations in how the musicians play each of their parts? Can you hear how particular elements float in and out of the song to keep the sound changing?

LISTENING GUIDE

0:00 | Introduction The song begins with a short descending melodic line played by the keyboards, followed by the entrance of the entire band including bass, drums, keyboards, and guitar. The band plays a continuously repeating vamp on an E minor chord. In the second eight measures, we can hear the addition of saxophone and the unique tone of the tubular bells. Listen to how the rhythm changes near the end of this section. The band suddenly shifts from a funky disco-inspired swing to a pattern that places all the emphasis on the downbeat (the one of each measure). It then quickly returns to the disco groove.

0:32 | Verse 1 Harry's voice enters in a high register as she sings a breathy melody over the band. Just listen to the subtle shifts in the sound and rhythms of Clem Burke's fantastic playing.

1:00 | Chorus It's pretty easy to tell that this is the chorus because it features the only real chord change in the entire song. The band now plays F, A, G, B, followed by F, A, C, G, and back to E minor as Harry sings the word rapture. You will also hear that the straight downbeat rhythmic pattern that showed up at the end of the introduction has become the basis for the majority of the chorus.

1:17 | Verse 2

1:44 | Chorus

2:02 | Instrumental Break This instrumental break is very important to the song. It serves as a musical transition from the new wave rock of the first two minutes to the hip hop–inspired second half. Hip hop DJs in the Bronx in the 1970s used to play sections like this on their record players, repeating it over and over in a musical loop, while MCs would come up to the microphone to rap their rhymes.

2:11 | Harry Raps As the band continues to play the break music, Harry begins to rap. She references a number of people who were popular in the hip hop scene in the Bronx including DJ Grandmaster Flash and Fab Five Freddy. Can you hear how different her vocal timbre and delivery are in this section compared to the first part of the song?

3:23 | Saxophone Solo The saxophone plays over the break music. Notice how the looped and effected percussion sounds drop out in the middle to make it sound more like a live band.

4:34 | Harry Raps II Harry enters a second rap as the music begins to fade and fall apart behind her. With her last words, "And now he only eats guitars," the music moves into a guitar solo, and the band begins to get louder again.

4:55 | Guitar Solo The guitar solo comes to a climax at 5:18 when the band plays through the chord changes from the chorus. This also helps to bring the whole band back into the opening groove of the song.

5:46 | Guitar and Sax Solos In this final section, the guitar and sax solo over the music of the introduction as the song fades out.

DAVID BOWIE

Played: **ROCK/GLAM ROCK/ART ROCK/NEW WAVE**

⊸ PLAYLIST ⊸

"Space Oddity" (1969)

"Changes" (1972)

"Ziggy Stardust" (1972)

"The Jean Genie" (1973)

"Rebel Rebel" (1974)

"Fame" (1975)

"Warszawa" (1977)

"Heroes" (1977)

"Ashes to Ashes" (1980)

"Let's Dance" (1983)

"Day in Day Out" (1987)

"I'm Afraid of Americans" (1997)

"Seven" (1997)

"(You Will) Set the World on Fire" (2013)

David Bowie, 1978

David Bowie has been a key figure in the history of rock and roll since the late 1960s. His constant drive to evolve, reinvent, and even disguise himself has led to a musical career that has touched on various musical sounds and brought him popularity with different audiences. From a very early age Bowie was interested in American rock and roll music, and he formed his first band at the age of fifteen. His art school background led him to peruse various opportunities in acting and music (fun fact: he appears as the antagonist in the 1986 Jim Henson movie *Labyrinth*—great fun for the whole family). His interest in theater led him to form an impressive array of alter egos for his musical live performances, and a number of these characters even became stand-ins for Bowie himself on recordings. For example, the album *The Rise and Fall of Ziggy Stardust and the Spiders from Mars* (1972) is a concept album in which Bowie plays the character Ziggy Stardust, and the live performances for the record featured Bowie dressing and acting like Ziggy on stage. He has continued to experiment with diverse musical sounds including soul, funk, glam rock, alternative rock, and electronic music, at the same time using various fashion looks from new romantic style to MTV-era pop star.

HISTORICAL FACT/SOCIAL CONNECTIONS

Bowie is always trying to push rock music in a new direction, while at the same time trying to create songs that will appeal to a wide audience. This means that he often takes something people know and combines it with something they don't, or at least something they don't remember much. In 1983, for the *Let's Dance* album, Bowie and producer Nile Rodgers (of Chic) used the idea of dance music as their guiding light. For each song on the album this concept played out in a slightly different way. "Modern Love" sounds like an early rock and roll song complete with a saxophone solo. "China Girl" sounds like a post-punk song, which it actually was; Bowie had cowritten it for Iggy Pop's 1977 album *The Idiot*. "Shake It" sounds like an '80s song by Prince. But all of these are presented with the sheen of new wave rock to help tie them together into one unified album. Take a listen to the record and see if you can hear how it works.

SONG FACTS: "LET'S DANCE" (1983)

Written by David Bowie

Released on EMI Records, 1983

The album *Let's Dance* features an interesting assortment of musicians including producer/guitarist Nile Rodgers, blues rock guitarist Stevie Ray Vaughan, and session drummer Tony Thompson. The band captures the sound of '80s new wave music while infusing it with elements of other kinds of popular dance music. Bowie had commented how he thought the song "Let's Dance" was a kind of experiment, and not much different from the ideas he worked on for his previous album *Scary Monsters* (1980) and its hit song "Ashes to Ashes." But what Bowie could not have predicted was that the new record became so successful that it actually helped to define the sound of new wave rock for most of the mid-1980s.

TRY THIS AT HOME

Bowie often adopts particular fashion styles to match the sound of a new record. Have some fun as a family by coming up with your own rock star fashions. You can turn this into a game by setting everyone up in a room with a pad and some paper. Then play a song out loud so everyone can hear. Have everyone in the room try to design a fashion style they imagine for the musicians.

"LET'S DANCE"

LISTENING GUIDE

For this guide, make sure you are listening to the shorter 4-minute radio single edit and not the longer 7-minute version from the album *Let's Dance*. Like Roxy Music, Bowie doesn't quite follow the rules of the pop song that he sets up here, and it is that kind of tug of war and pull between what the music does and what we expect that makes it great . . . like the fact that there is no real chorus.

0:00 | Introduction This song begins with a vocal and instrumental buildup that is taken right from classic rock and roll. Think of the bridge section of the song "Twist and Shout" by the Beatles where John, Paul, and George harmonize on a repeated chord to build up the sound.

0:09 | Instrumental Introduction The opening of the song segues into a more traditional instrumental section that establishes the groove of the song. This is the perfect moment to pay attention to the beautiful production work that creates a unique sonic landscape.

Drums: The kick and snare drum play with what is called a gated effect that makes them sound large with a swelling sound, but it also cuts them off with an unnatural ending. You can also hear the sound of pitched wood blocks.

Bass: The bass guitar actually plays the main melodic material of this section and foreshadows the melody Bowie will sing in the verses.

Saxophones and Guitar: The horns and guitar play a repeated pattern that shifts with the chord changes. Listen closely and you can hear the echo put on these instruments working in synchronization with the tempo of the song.

0:26 | Verse 1 When the verse begins, you will notice that the vocal parts are done in a reverse call and response. The backing vocals first shout, "Let's Dance" to which Bowie says "Put on your red shoes and dance the blues." This pattern continues throughout the entire verse.

1:00 | Bridge The music changes as instruments either drop out or hold out their notes longer. The rhythm also has a dramatic change here as the funky swing of the verse is replaced with a pattern that is much straighter: 1, 2, + 3, 4.

1:16 | Build The music returns to the same vocal build that opened the song, and like the opening, it pushes the music back to the funk groove.

1:31 | Musical Break The backing singers shout "Let's dance" while the guitar threatens to enter into a solo, but it does not.

1:48 | Verse 2 The music in the second verse is almost the same as the first, but listen to the difference in Bowie's voice. His voice is much softer here. You can hear his breath—the sounds vulnerable until he shouts "under the moonlight, the serious moonlight."

2:22 | Bridge

2:38 | Build

2:52 | Musical Break

3:08 | Verse 3 In the third and final short verse, Bowie shouts the whole thing in a variation of the melody from the first two.

3:25 | Guitar Solo Things get a bit chaotic as the music begins to fade out.

DEVO

Played: PUNK/ART ROCK/NEW WAVE/EXPERIMENTAL POP

⊸ PLAYLIST ⊷

"Mechanical Man" (1978)

"(I Can't Get No) Satisfaction" (1978)

"Jocko Homo" (1978)

"Whip It" (1980)

"Working in a Coal Mine" (1981)

"Through Being Cool" (1981)

"Big Mess" (1982)

"Here to Go" (1984)

"Disco Dancer" (1988)

"Watch Us Work It" (2007)

"On the Inside" (2013)

Devo in the music video for "Satisfaction"

Although most people probably remember Devo as the band who wore red flowerpots on their heads, their history and music is actually quite fascinating and noteworthy (for example, those flowerpot hats were called "energy domes" by the band). The concept for the band Devo first began when a number of art students at Kent State University started to experiment with a concept they called "de-evolution." Their idea was to create artworks that represented less-refined forms of art, not progressing forward as avant-garde artists wanted to do. The concept was also tied to a tragic real-life event that inspired them to create music in the first place—the Kent State shootings of May 4, 1970, in which four students were killed and several others wounded at an anti-war rally. Devo began to make music that suggested the world was moving backwards in the modern age, that things were getting worse in their opinion, not better. The famous lineup of the band came about in 1972 and featured two sets of brothers, Bob (guitar) and Gerald Casale (bass), and Bob (guitar) and Mark (keyboards) Mothersbaugh, along with Alan Myers (drums). The name of the band came directly from their early concept of de-evolution (Devo), and their punk-inspired sound mixed keyboards with metronomic rhythms and a unique vocal timbre to create a quintessentially new wave sound.

HISTORICAL FACT/SOCIAL CONNECTIONS

Devo's lyrics are filled with dark humor, and often play with the idea of de-evolution. The song "Jocko Homo" from their first album explains the concept, suggesting that humanity is regressing, that we are not much more than monkeys in business suits. Have your family think about why a band like Devo might think that during the mid-1970s. Explain what happened at the Kent State shootings and think about how that might have affected students who were on campus at the time. Then think about the 1980 song "Freedom of Choice." What do you think Devo is trying to say in the lyrics? Why do you think they talk about a dog that is confronted with a choice to make and as a result can only run around in circles? What is our freedom of choice in the land of the free? What might Devo want us to do about it?

NG FACTS: "WHIP IT" (1980)

Written by Gerald Casale and
Mark Mothersbaugh
Released on Warner Brothers Records,
980

While the song has a sincere message
at heart—the American work ethic that
says you should solve a problem when
it arises—what I really love about this
song is the humor and wordplay. In
the chorus, the lyrics suggest that one
should look at a problem and "whip it."
take care of it). The next line, however,
lets us know that it cream sits out too
long on the counter, you need to "whip
it." For those who want to read a little
deeper into the meaning of the song,
you can think about how it relates to
freedom of Choice. The record rails
against corporate greed and the values
of the '80s "me" generation, which
Devo often referred to as monkeys in
business suits.

DESTINATIONS

See where Devo got their start in
northeast Ohio. Visit the Kent State
University campus and see a memorial
to the shootings located at the May 4
visitors' center that is free and open to
the public. The exhibits talk about the
political and social landscape of the time
and feature a detailed account of what
happened that day. Visit the music scene
in neighboring Akron, Ohio, where Devo
played many of their first gigs. There's
still a great music scene there that has
been the home to Chrissie Hynde of the
Pretenders, and the Black Keys.

"WHIP IT"

LISTENING GUIDE

The structure of this song is a pretty straightforward verse-chorus model. The
experimentation comes from the syncopated rhythms and broken, chopped-up
melodies. The sound and rhythmic patterns of the drums were heavily influenced
by German bands like Neu! and Kraftwerk. The bass line and guitar riff exhibit a
connection to American rock and even a touch of R&B.

0:00 | Introduction The song opens with
the drum set playing fast hi-hat sounds with
a metronomic kick and snare pattern. This
particular sound comes from German rock bands.
The bass (played on a Moog synthesizer) and
guitar enter the song playing the infectious stop-
and start melodic riff. Another synthesizer adds
the descending "bing, bong, boom" melodic line
and the percussive whip sound.

0:18 | Verse 1 Mark Mothersbaugh enters
singing the main melody. Listen to the sound
of his voice. It is not what we might call a great
singing voice, especially due to the nasal timbre it
has. He jumps back and forth between a higher
shouted tone and a lower spoken tone. It is this
unusual sound that makes this song (and most of
Devo's music) so recognizable.
The opening words of the song say to "crack the
whip and give the past a slip." It's a clever use
of the workplace "crack the whip" image used in
reverse—suggesting that we should "slip" out of
the modern trajectory of more hours and less pay
and find a new model.

0:31 | Chorus The music stays basically the
same as the verse. If you listen carefully, you hear
that there is a new guitar lick played in the second
part of each vocal phrase. Mothersbaugh sings in
call and response with the background vocals.

0:43 | Postchorus This section really stands out
from the rest of the song. The drums don't stop
and then keep playing that same pattern! The
synthesizer plays a sirenlike sound in the upper
register that moves back and forth between the
left and right speakers.

0:58 | Verse 2

Note how the vocals trade back and forth
with the bass and guitar. Listen to how the
first thing in the section is the bass and guitar
playing a short "bum, bum, boomp" motive.
Then when Mothersbaugh sings "Now whip it,"
the instruments are silent. The bass and guitar
then play the same motive but starting on a
new note, followed by Mothersbaugh shouting,
"into shape." This back and forth continues
through the entire section.

1:10 | Chorus This chorus is very similar to
the first, but it now features the guitar playing
power chords that sound like '70s rock. This
helps to give this chorus more energy and
separate it from the verse.

1:22 | Instrumental Break This section is
very similar to the instrumental introduction
of the song, but with a bit more motion in the
bass line, and a repeated sonar ping sound in
the high synthesizer part.

1:41 | Verse 3

1:54 | Chorus

2:05 | Postchorus (X 2)

2:32 | Outro

DEPECHE MODE

Played: **SYNTH-POP**

⊣ PLAYLIST ⊢

"Just Can't Get Enough" (1981)

"See You" (1982)

"Everything Counts" (1983)

"People Are People" (1984)

"New Dress" (1986)

"Strange Love" (1987)

"Enjoy the Silence" (1990)

"Walking in My Shoes" (1993)

"It's No Good" (1997)

"Precious" (2005)

"In Sympathy" (2009)

Depeche Mode on Top of the Pops, *1981*

The band Depeche Mode began in October 1980 when Andrew Fletcher, David Gahan, Martin Gore, and Vince Clarke recorded a three-song demo in order to obtain a gig at the London nightclub the Bridgehouse, which featured new wave and electronic music. Like many of the other bands in this chapter, Depeche Mode was interested in the ways that music and style could mix—in fact, the name of the band comes from a French magazine that translates into English as "fast fashion." They were one of the first bands to blend metallic percussion sounds with synthesizer tones and pop song structures. Their lyrics spoke of universal human concerns such as relationships, jobs, faith, love, anger, and hope. While they also hinted at politics and philosophy, their focus was always on the personal consequences of living in the modern world. Founding member Clarke left at the end of 1981 after the release of their first major album on Mute Records and was replaced by synthesizer guru Alan Wilder. They continue to evolve their sound today, often bringing in more traditional rock instrumentation such as electric guitars and live drums.

Depeche Mode live in 1986

HISTORICAL FACT/SOCIAL CONNECTIONS

So far we have seen several examples of musicians making use of synthesizers to create music, but the development of synth-pop in the early 1980s was different because it made the synthesizer the center. Some of the early experimental bands that used synthesizers included Kraftwerk in Germany and the Yellow Magic Orchestra in Japan. At the dawn of the 1980s, a number of new groups from England revolutionized fully synthesized music by making it unapologetically pop. The groups used drum machines and sequencers to create rhythmic music from a limited number of melodic elements, and featuring complex timbres and interlocking patterns

SONG FACTS: "PEOPLE ARE PEOPLE" (1984)

Written by Martin Gore

Released on Mute Records, 1984

This song was originally released as a single in 1984. The song was written by Martin Gore, who was quickly becoming the main songwriter of the group following the departure of Vince Clarke. Gore's lyrics are straightforward and ask the listener to think about why hate and violence exist in the world. The song acknowledges the differences people have around the world—skin color, religion, etc.—but asks us to see that we are all human underneath, despite our different needs and desires. Use this as an opportunity to talk with your family about the many ways we differ, and how we can teach tolerance and understanding.

TRY THIS AT HOME

Today, you can create an entire range of synthesized music on your computer, tablet, or even your phone. For this activity, you will not only need some good electronic sounds, but you'll put them together into a song. If you are feeling like this might be too much for you, download something like the app Figure. This inexpensive app lets you pick a sound for three different instruments: drums, bass, and lead. You can program what notes each will play and how they interact. You can even mix it and save it as an audio file. Once you get the hang of that, try moving on to Garage Band, and eventually something like Reason—which lets you work on the same software as many current pop stars.

"PEOPLE ARE PEOPLE"

LISTENING GUIDE

This song was recorded in West Berlin, which greatly influenced its sound. The members of Depeche Mode had been listening to German industrial music by groups like Einstürzende Neubauten, who used sheet metal and sledgehammers to create a junkyard symphony. Depeche Mode was working with producer Gareth Jones, who was known for his ability to work with new digital sampling keyboards. These instruments allowed you to record short snippets of sound, manipulate them, and play them back via a synthesizer-style keyboard. This metallic sampling manipulation became the basis of the song "People Are People."

0:00 | Percussion Introduction The sampled percussion and drum machine establish the factorylike aspect of the song right from the start. Listen to how the reverb effect on the drum machine makes it sound like the music is playing in a large space. After four measures two synthesizer sounds enter. The first is a low tone that plays the bass line, and the second is a springlike sound that plays a high-pitched melody.

0:32 | Chorus The music settles into something much closer to a pop song with the factory sounds making up the percussion section. Check out the cool vocal "dum dum dum" sounds played by the synthesizer at the end of the chorus. The vocal sound here is really interesting and is actually a combination of two voices. Lead singer Dave Gahan sings in a lower register while Martin Gore sings in a high smooth falsetto. When the two of them sing in the chorus, they each sing a different melodic line. This has become a signature sound of Depeche Mode.

0:53 | Verse 1 The metallic percussion stops and is replaced by synthesizer sounds. This lets the energy of the music pull back in the verse and allows Gahan to take center stage. The timbre of his voice is recognizable, and works really well over the synthesized background.

1:11 | Prechorus Even though the tempo stays the same, it might feel a little slower, as the instruments begin to strike and hold out single notes. The vocal in this section is sung by Gore in his high-pitched soft tone and creates a good contrast to Gahan's rough rhythmic voice in the verses.

1:18 | Chorus

1:38 | Bridge This bridge uses a melodic vocal idea from the prechorus section. Both Gahan and Gore sing the lyric "help me understand" as the metallic percussion and drum machine sounds from the opening play behind them.

2:02 | Verse 2 This verse features additional rhythmic synthesizer sounds.

2:19 | Prechorus

2:26 | Chorus

2:48 | Prechorus Buildup The rhythm of this section shifts from the factory-inspired backbeat that has been playing for most of the song and begins to pound out a single pulse—bang, bang, bang, bang. The synthesizer still plays in 4/4 time as multiple copies of Gahan and Gore's voices sing various lines from the song in a polyphonic texture.

3:37 | Unwinding Spring Sound and Fadeout

Played: **POST PUNK / INDIE ROCK / ALTERNATIVE ROCK**

~ PLAYLIST ~

"Hand in Glove" (1983)

"What Difference Does It Make" (1983)

"Heaven Knows I'm Miserable Now" (1984)

"How Soon Is Now?" (1984)

"The Boy with the Thorn in His Side" (1985)

"Nowhere Fast" (1985)

"Barbarism Begins At Home" (1985)

"Panic" (1986)

"Ask" (1986)

"Sheila Take a Bow" (1987)

"Last Night I Dreamt That Somebody Loved Me" (1987)

The Smiths perform on the Oxford Road Show, 1985

The Smiths (clockwise from left: Morrissey, Johnny Marr, Mike Joyce, and Andy Rourke)

The Smiths formed in Manchester, England, in 1982, and by 1987 they had already broken up. Within those five short years, they helped to revolutionize post punk and turn it into what we now know as modern indie rock. The group was a rock-style quartet featuring Morrissey (vocals), Johnny Marr (guitar), Andy Rourke (bass), and Mike Joyce (drums), and their sound was deeply rooted in 1960s guitar rock (like the Byrds) and post punk (like the Cure). This separated them from the many synthesizer-based bands filling the airwaves in the 1980s. Lead singer Morrissey once commented that he picked the name of the band because it was ordinary sounding, and that he wanted the band to speak for the ordinary people of the world. The sound of their music helped to transform what were fairly dark gothic topics and lyrics into relatable tragedies of the everyday person, stories filled with a sense of loneliness and sadness.

HISTORICAL FACT/SOCIAL CONNECTIONS

Bands like the Smiths proved that rock could still be a voice for something important in the more commercial musical space of the 1980s. While much of their music was dark and brooding, talking about inner conflicts and love gone astray, they also began to take a stand on particular topics—especially lead singer Morrissey. The turning point for the band was the 1985 album *Meat Is Murder,* in which Morrissey took a strong position regarding his beliefs in a vegetarian lifestyle. The lyrics of the album's title song are an intense depiction of the slaughter of animals and the cooking of meat. The topics on the album also look at other political issues of the time. For example the song "Nowhere Fast" is an existentialist condemnation of the modern world that focuses its disgust on the royal family of England and the British class system.

SONG FACTS: "HOW SOON IS NOW?" (1984)

Written by Johnny Marr and Morrissey
Released on Rough Trade Records,
January 1985

I think this song is amazing (I still remember the first time I heard it), Sire Records owner Seymour Stein once called it the "Stairway to Heaven" of the 1980s. It's funny to juxtapose that with the fact that this song was originally a B-side, and was even left off of the album *Meat Is Murder* when it first came out. But the song's trancelike vibe and 12-minute running time helped to make a smash in underground dance clubs, and it soon took on a life of its own.

TRY THIS AT HOME

Now that you are almost at the end of the book, hopefully you have begun to gain an appreciation for the history of rock and roll music, and both you and your family have begun to develop a list of your own favorite tunes. So why not share it with some of your friends and neighbors? Set up a space where everyone can come and relax and listen to the music you enjoy. You can even come up with some ideas to make it a fun party. For example: play a classic album from beginning to end; have people talk about the history or sound of every song you play; have guests share memories of songs they know. You can even ask some of your guests to bring their own music to play. But most of all, don't forget to make it about the music. Try to encourage people to talk about what they hear.

"HOW SOON IS NOW?"

LISTENING GUIDE

In many ways, this song does not sound like a typical Smiths song. It is awash in reverb and delay and the main vibrato guitar riff plays over and over like a mantra. Morrissey's crooning vocals are filled with longing, telling listeners that he is a man who is lonely and can't find a way to break out of his own shy demeanor. The constant guitar playing on a single chord becomes the monotony of a life lived in isolation, except for the few moments in which Morrissey breaks out of his stupor and allows himself to dream.

0:00 | Percussion Introduction This song has a single guitar riff at its core—everything else comes from it or plays against it. It is a repeated rhythmic pattern strumming on an E chord. That rhythmic pattern is very similar to the famous Bo Diddley beat (1, 2, 3—1, 2). The sound of Johnny Marr's guitar is rich and textured. Everything you hear is the sound of one guitar, but duplicated, altered, and layered back on itself so you can hear a full chorus of vibrating guitar sounds—amazing!

0:08 | Band Introduction The entrance of the full band is announced by a ringing slide guitar tone that bends up and then down. Listen to the drums and you can hear that famous '80s reverb/gated sound, especially in the snare drum. The bass guitar walks around the notes of the scale, sometimes highlighting the sound of the guitar, and at other times playing within the small gaps.

0:20 | Verse 1 Morrissey begins with a clear open timbre in his voice and a sense of confidence as he sings. That suddenly fades in the second half of the verse as he begins to mumble and his voice gets lost in the sound of the music.

0:42 | Chorus The rhythmic guitar continues but a new second guitar enters playing a new progression with the bass. You can really hear some of the crazy noodling sounds of that new guitar at the end of the chorus. Morrissey's voice pushes into a powerful higher register as he talks back to those who put him down as he pleads for love and understanding.

1:08 | Instrumental Break

1:19 | Verse 2 Listen to the variations that Morrissey makes to the melodic line of the verse. For example, this time the word "air" hangs, quite literally in the air.

1:42 | Chorus

2:09 | Instrumental Break

2:42 | Chorus

3:10 | Instrumental Break This break is very similar to the previous ones, but they add another new sound to keep things fresh. I'm not quite sure what that sound is. It sounds like a mix of guitar and percussion, and it also has the timbre of a sound that the Yamaha DX-7 synthesizer used to make called FM Bells. Either way, it really sticks out of the previous texture and brings new life to the song at the midway point.

3:44 | Chorus

4:10 | Instrumental Break

4:43 | Chorus/Instrumental

5:01 | Break As this break begins, the music cuts out as if it hit a brick wall. The only thing that remains is the amazing rhythmic guitar and a scratchy guitar noise. The song then begins to build itself back up. Drums first, then bass. Then the slide guitar and the FM Bells sound.

5:45 | Chorus

6:11 | Instrumental Break The instrumental music returns as the song fades out.

R.E.M.

Played: **ALTERNATIVE ROCK**

R.E.M., 1983

R.E.M. was the band that made the final jump from post punk and new wave to what would become a broader marketing category called alternative rock. R.E.M. didn't sound like the emotional darkness of the Smiths and didn't use synthesizers like Depeche Mode. They used elements of American roots music and didn't try to hide the fact that they were from Athens, Georgia (many American bands at the time tried to sound British). The group consisted of Michael Stipe (vocals), Peter Buck (guitar), Mike Mills (bass), and Bill Berry (drums). Despite the fact that the band came from a postpunk background, their music is often mid-tempo, and many of their most famous songs are ballads (like "Everybody Hurts"). While Michael Stipe's lyrics are often lauded for their intense introspection and juxtaposition of images, it is also a common observation that few people ever understand exactly what he is saying. The sound of the words was what was most important to him, and the music is all the better for it.

R.E.M., 1986

HISTORICAL FACT/SOCIAL CONNECTIONS

For much of their career, R.E.M. was signed to the independent record label I.R.S. that was owned by Miles Copeland (brother of Stewart Copeland from the band the Police). The rise of independent record labels in the 1980s parallels the emergence of independent labels in the 1950s that helped to give rise to rock and roll music. In the 1980s, these smaller labels allowed many bands to make records that had no chance of being recorded by the major labels that were recording arena rock bands and pop artists. The smaller "indie" labels allowed musicians the freedom to do what they wanted and experiment with their sound without worrying about the need to have a hit song on the radio. Much of this indie label music did eventually find a home on radio. College rock radio stations played music by new, and undiscovered artists. This also led to a growing college tour scene for bands that traveled from one college-town to the next to play on campus or in small clubs.

"IT'S THE END OF THE WORLD AS WE KNOW IT (AND I FEEL FINE)"

SONG FACTS: "IT'S THE END OF THE WORLD AS WE KNOW IT (AND I FEEL FINE)" (1987)

Written by Bill Berry, Peter Buck, Mike Mills, and Michael Stipe

Released on I.R.S. Records, November 1987

As exciting and original as this song sounds, there is no denying that it takes its inspiration from the Bob Dylan classic "Subterranean Homesick Blues." Both songs rattle through what appears to be a fast stream-of-consciousness set of lyrics that do make a little more sense if you slow down and look at them all. In the case of R.E.M., the words fly forth as a mish-mash of current events and dreamlike images. In fact, Stipe has said that the majority of the words in the song were either things he heard on television or images he saw in his dreams. The end result is a song that predicts the end of the world (earthquakes, hurricanes, snakes, and combat sites), and is presented to us with the speed and fractured nature of the modern world (birthday party; cheesecake; jellybean; and then; boom). And let's not forget that this was written before the Internet was in all our homes and pockets!

LISTENING GUIDE

The rapid-fire lyrics of Stipe take center stage for most of this song as the band cranks out the postpunk-sounding background. Listen for the ways that the instruments and backing vocals change what and how they play over the song's 4 minutes.

0:00 | Snare Introduction What's a great way to announce the beginning of the song? A series of snare drum rolls. It also has the added effect of making us think about a military march, which might be suggestive of some of the end-of-the-world situations mentioned in the song.

0:03 | Verse 1 The verse starts all at once and right away, as if it was sitting behind the scenes waiting to spring out when you pressed play. The drums play a rock and roll backbeat, but the overall sound of what Berry is playing has a very country music feel to it. Mills's bass follows the chord progression while it plays its own set of melodic lines. Buck's guitar has a fairly clean tone in the beginning that gets more distorted when he begins to strum the chords.

0:49 | Chorus While the lyrics tell us that it is the end of the world, the music actually feels pretty happy. The main melody is a great sing-along. After all, the point of the song is that the world may be ending from biblical disasters, military aggression, or even just the complete breakdown of society from the postmodern meaninglessness of pop culture . . . but in the end, "I feel fine."

1:08 | Verse 2 The band moves back into the music of the verse and Stipe begins another rant. If you listen, you can hear that there is actually more than one copy of his voice singing the lyrics.

1:32 | Chorus The band is really rocking by this point. This time there is a great countermelody in the background that sings "It's time I had some time alone." This line is quite funny in the way it tries to take an optimistic look at the fact that everyone on the planet is going to be wiped out.

1:48 | Bridge A musical break features some kind of whistle/recorder sound, and for the first time we can hear that a piano has joined the band. The song has been making such a subtle buildup for the last two minutes that you may not have noticed it, but listen to how much more aggressive it sounds now compared to the beginning.

2:05 | Chorus The bridge runs right into the chorus at full steam. The mix actually does something interesting here. Listen to the way that the countermelody from the last chorus, "had some time alone," takes the lead. There are also a lot more people singing at this point, compared to the first chorus.

2:22 | Verse 3 Another rapid-fire verse that is interrupted this time by the fact that the entire band stops playing as Stipe shouts, "Leonard Bernstein." This creates a great musical moment where you are suddenly forced to realize the hectic pace and sonic bombardment of the song at the point when it stops.

2:36 | Chorus

2:56 | Break

3:00 | Chorus In this chorus, the only instruments playing are acoustic guitar and tambourine. The focus is the polyphony of the various voices singing one of the two melodies from the chorus.

3:18 | Chorus The song ends with a big, full-on chorus that fades out as the voices keep singing.

U2

Played: **POST PUNK/ALTERNATIVE ROCK/ROCK**

U2, 1980

Named after the Cold War–era U2 spy plane and hailing from Dublin, Ireland, this band got its start in 1976 playing postpunk rock and went on to be one of the most successful bands of all time. Their distinctive sound comes from the unique playing of its four tight-knit members: Bono (vocals), the Edge (guitar), Adam Clayton (bass), and Larry Mullen Jr. (drums). Mullen plays the drums with a powerful touch that also projects the sense that he is in complete control of the proceedings. Clayton's bass serves a dual function. On one hand, it completes the rhythm section and creates the foundation, and on the other it serves as its own melodic line (much in the tradition of melodic bass players like John Entwistle and Chris Squire). The Edge has always been responsible for the signature sound of the band. His clean electric guitar playing strives for texture over melody, and his rhythmic playing is frequently processed by effects that allow him to create a mass of sound—take a listen to a song like "New Year's Day" (1983). Bono's strong voice always places him at the center of the proceedings. His ability to sing across a wide vocal range and control the timbre of his voice allows him to project a raw sense of emotion to his audience—listen to "Wire" (1984).

Bono performs during the Vertigo tour, 2005

HISTORICAL FACT/SOCIAL CONNECTIONS

Now that we're at the end of the book, we can have some fun debating the history of rock and roll. There are many rock critics and fans who claim that U2 might just be the last great rock and roll band. What do they mean by that? Well, most of them want to imply that the era of the rock band ended in the twentieth century. After that time, pop music (meaning radio-friendly music) and hip hop took over the mantel as the most popular styles of popular music. There is some argument to be made for that; the sounds of hip hop are certainly the most dominant sounds of youth culture as I sit here and write this book. But the idea of a rock band is not dead; in fact there are many great bands around today. What some people mean when they say U2 is the last great rock and roll band is that they find it hard to imagine a band who could have such a long and creative career these days, and that is certainly more difficult to accomplish now than it was in the 1980s. But let's be hopeful. People have pronounced rock and roll dead many times. U2 is a great band, but I have a feeling that they won't be the last.

SONG FACTS: "WHERE THE STREETS HAVE NO NAME" (1987)

Written by U2

Released on Island Records, March 1987

…is song is the opening track from the …um *The Joshua Tree*, so it has a really …ng build at the start to pull you into …e record. The album was produced …y Brian Eno (who played on the early …xy Music albums) and Daniel Lanois. …e sound of the music is just fantastic. …ch instrument can be heard clearly in …e mellow moments of the song, but …gether, they add up to a musical wall …sound during the big choruses.

TRY THIS AT HOME

…t's save the world and make it a better …ace—really. We can't do it unless we start by believing that it is possible. …at's how I hear the lyrics of "Where …e Streets Have No Name": as a call for …arity, for peace, and to hope. A place …ere there are no physical barriers or …eological concepts dividing us. It's a …opian idea to be sure, but one that is …old as rock and roll itself. It's what …e Beatles sang about in "All You Need …Love" and Depeche Mode in "People …e People." It's what makes us come …gether at the best and the worst of …es. But it all starts with each of us. …t's try to think more about how we can …me together and less about how to …ar us apart. Let's not just listen to the …ories of poverty, hunger, pain, and strife … the news, and read about them on …e Internet as we race along in our daily …es. Let's stop for just a moment and do …mething about it.

LISTENING GUIDE

"WHERE THE STREETS HAVE NO NAME"

0:00 | Introduction The song starts with swelling organ sounds that sound far away, like they are playing in a cave just below where we are listening. There's some other sound, like high-pitched birds, swirling around as well. As the organ sound comes closer to us, it gets clearer and the other sound drops away.

At the 40-second mark, the Edge's guitar enters, repeating a short motif that sounds like it came from a piece of music by composer Philip Glass.

1:10 | Buildup The bass and drums enter and give us the feeling that the song is finally about to begin. The kick drum pulses the beat as roto-toms and cymbals build up the tension. The bass plays along with the organ and guitar in a galloping rhythm. Suddenly they all begin to play short repeated notes as the music builds to a crescendo.

1:48 | Verse 1 Take note: We're almost 2 minutes in before the first word is sung. The music settles into a nice groove established by the bass and drums. The guitar plays a scratchy, almost nonpitched, rhythm that is accomplished by holding your palm over the strings to stop them from ringing. Every once and a while, the Edge removes his hand to let the chord ring out. Can you hear it? Bono sings the lyrics of the verse in a very start-and-stop manner, but soon breaks into long melodic phrases. His voice is in a high register but it has a lot of character to it. Listen to what some might call the "grain" of the voice, the scratches in his inflection, and the quick vibrato at the end of his phrases.

2:18 | Verse 2 The drums start to play a backbeat using the snare drum.

2:50 | Chorus The music suddenly builds up as the guitar shifts from the percussive sound to a high-pitched, melodic motive, Mullen establish an even more dominant backbeat than he has played before. Bono launches into a highly emotional vocal melody that pushes up higher and higher and then starts to fall back down by the end of the chorus. It creates the sense that the high point of the chorus was in the middle of it.

3:20 | Verse 3 This verse is close to the first two, except for the fact that there is a much bigger buildup to the next chorus.

3:50 | Double Chorus This chorus begins full steam with all cylinders firing. Bono reaches up even higher in the emotional power of his voice—to the point that the song itself won't let the chorus stop. The music continues to push into a second full chorus. Make no mistake; the band does this with the complete knowledge that this moment will push us, the listener, into total rhythmic, emotional, spiritual, and melodic ecstasy—fully in sync with the music. This is one of those great musical moments that can give you goosebumps if you listen to it with your undivided attention (or if you're singing along in the car racing down the highway—to each his/her own).

4:53 | Outro The music breaks down into a simplified organ/bass/guitar sound. The song ends as a guitar motive echoes and fades into the distance.

Rock and Roll Hall of Fame, Cleveland, Ohio

⸜ ROCK DESTINATIONS ⸝

Now that you've almost reached the end of the book (make sure to check out the additional playlists), you can get your family out on the road and visit some of the many rock music destinations listed here. You can add one of these trips to a vacation you are already taking, or you can plan a trip just for the purpose of experiencing rock history. Take note that some of the destinations mentioned are located in the same part of the United States or even the same city (such as Memphis).

The list of destinations wouldn't be complete without a trip to the house that rock built on the shore of Lake Erie in Cleveland, Ohio: The Rock and Roll Hall of Fame and Museum. The Museum offers six floors of exhibits that span the entire history of rock and roll from its roots to current musicians. Most of the major exhibits are focused on the inductees of the Hall of Fame, but you can also find a lot of exciting artifacts from other artists as well. Plan to spend a full day there since just the films alone can occupy the better part of your day. If you look on the website (www.rockhall.com), you may even be able to time your visit so you can participate in one of the many free events the Rock Hall hosts. While you are there, Cleveland is also home to some great food, sports teams (baseball, football, and basketball), and a host of other museums and shopping.

Chapter 1: Rock & Roll Basics
LAB 1: ELVIS PRESLEY
Originally Recorded By
If you like the music of Elvis, go take a listen to the musicians who originally recorded some of his songs.

Arthur "Big Boy" Crudup, "That's All Right" (1946)
Arthur Crudup was born in 1905. He lived in Mississippi and later moved north to Chicago, and because of this, his music contains elements of both Delta blues from the Deep South and electrified blues from Chicago.

Bill Monroe, "Blue Moon of Kentucky" (1946)
Not many musicians can be said to have single-handedly developed a new style of music, but in the case of Bill Monroe and bluegrass, it's true. Monroe's voice is accompanied by his dynamic mandolin picking, fiddle, and the playing of guitarist Lester Flatt and banjo player Earl Scruggs.

Wyonnie Harris, "Good Rockin' Tonight" (1947)
A classic jump blues (up-tempo blues) recorded at King Records in Cincinnati, Ohio. Listen to the great horn parts played in response to Harris's voice. Want to go back even further? Have a listen to the version of the song by Roy Brown earlier in 1947.

Junior Parker, "Mystery Train" (1953)
Originally recorded by Parker for the Sun Records label in 1953, Phillips liked the song so much he asked Elvis to record it in 1955. Listen to how Elvis tried to capture the same vocal sound as Parker.

LAB 2: CHUCK BERRY
Originally Recorded By
If you like the music of Chuck Berry, then go take a listen to the pop, country, jazz, and rhythm and blues music that helped to shape his signature sound.

Bob Wills and his Texas Playboys, "Ida Red" (1938)
This song is a traditional American folk song (we don't even know who wrote it). The recording by Bob Wills is performed in a Western swing style with some great fiddle playing. Berry's hit song "Maybellene" is an adaptation of this tune.

Charlie Christian (with Benny Goodman and his Orchestra), "Solo Flight" (1942)
Christian was a guitar player who was well known for performing in Benny Goodman's big band in the early 1940s. While playing with the band, he developed a style in which his guitar sounded like a horn, and many of his solos are played on one string with a strong rhythmic element.

Louis Jordan and his Tympany Five, "Ain't That Just Like a Woman" (1946)
Over the years, I have had the chance to talk to many early rock and roll musicians, and almost everyone will mention Louis Jordan and his guitar player Carl Hogan. In fact, Chuck Berry called Hogan one of his idols.

Nat King Cole, "Route 66" (1946)
This classic jazz tune written by Bobby Troup was first recorded by pop music star Nat King Cole, who sang and played piano. The sweet melodic sounds of Cole strongly influenced the young Chuck Berry.

LAB 3: FATS DOMINO
The Sounds of New Orleans
Fats Domino is just one of the many musicians who played rhythm and blues–based rock and roll in the city of New Orleans, so check out some of these other great piano players.

Professor Longhair, "Mardi Gras in New Orleans" (1949)
Professor Longhair's signature song uses a rhumba-inspired Latin rhythm and features piano, singing, and even whistling. The lyrics are about traveling to New Orleans to have a good time.

Smiley Lewis, "I Hear You Knockin'" (1955)
One of the great Bourbon Street boogie-woogie piano players who started recording in 1947 with songs like "Turn on Your Volume." This song was written by Dave Bartholomew and Earl King and has been recorded numerous times by other artists, including Fats Domino.

Allen Toussaint, "Java" (1958)
Toussaint worked as a songwriter and producer in New Orleans and helped to create some of the city's most famous music. This short instrumental captures the sonic spirit of the city and Toussaint's lively piano playing.

Dr. John, "Right Place Wrong Time" (1973)
Dr. John started as a session piano player in New Orleans but soon created his own funky version of the music he grew up with. The band playing with him on this song is the legendary New Orleans group the Meters, and the record was produced by Allen Toussaint.

LAB 4: JOHNNY CASH
Other Artists at Sun Records in Memphis
Johnny Cash and Elvis Presley both began their careers at Sun Records in Memphis, and so did a lot of other rock and roll musicians.

Jackie Brenston & His Delta Cats, "Rocket 88" (1951)
It's cheating a little to put this here, since the record actually was released by Chess Records, but Sam Phillips recorded the song in the Memphis Recording Service. It features Ike Turner and his band the Rhythm Kings as the backing group (yes, *that* Ike Turner).

Carl Perkins, "Blue Suede Shoes" (1956)
This famous song was written and originally recorded by Perkins, but a car accident caused his rising star to lose some momentum. The Elvis Presley version from 1957 is one of the best-known versions of the song.

Roy Orbison, "Ooby Dooby" (1956)
Orbison became famous for songs like "Crying," recorded for the Monument record label in the early 1960s, but he started by recording songs for Sun. This song is a fun one to sing along with (especially when I joke with my kids and change the lyrics to Scooby-Dooby!).

Jerry Lee Lewis, "Whole Lotta Shakin' Goin' On" (1957)
Known as "The Killer" for his wild style of piano playing (really—go look it up online), Lewis first recorded at Sun Records in 1956. This song was his first big hit. Check out the great piano solo, and listen carefully for the Sun Records echo that pervades the entire recording.

LAB 5: THE SHIRELLES
THE RISE OF THE GIRL GROUPS
During the late 1950s and early 1960s, vocal harmony groups consisting of all female members became popular and gave rise to the name girl groups. Take a listen to some of the best.

The Chantels, "Maybe" (1958)
The Chantels recorded their hits before there was such a label as girl group, but there can be no doubt that the sound of songs like this one set the stage for groups like the Shirelles.

The Ronettes, "Be My Baby" (1963)
Written by New York City Brill Building songwriters Jeff Barry and Ellie Greenwich along with producer Phil Spector, the music has Spector's trademark "wall of sound" (a large number of instruments playing all at once). Listen to how vocalist Ronnie Spector rises above the instrumentation to take center stage.

The Chiffons, "He's So Fine" (1963)
A fun song with great backing vocals that chant, "Doo-Lang, Doo-Lang, Doo-Lang." Now that you know the words, sing along (even if someone's watching).

The Shangri-Las, "Leader of the Pack" (1964)
The spoken dialogue and motorcycle sounds at the start of this song always pull me right into the drama of the story. The great melody and the musical arrangement keep me there.

LAB 6: FRANKIE LYMON AND THE TEENAGERS
EARLY ROCK AND ROLL VOCAL HARMONY
In the mid-1950s, many different musical sounds joined together under the umbrella term rock and roll, and one of the really important ingredients was the sound of African American groups performing rhythm and blues/gospel-inspired vocal harmony music.

The Ink Spots, "If I Didn't Care" (1939)
The Ink Spots of Indianapolis, Indiana, were one of the finest vocal harmony groups from the generation before rock and roll. A simple piano and guitar background supports the lush vocal parts.

The Orioles, "It's Too Soon to Know" (1948)
The Orioles are the link between the early vocal sound of groups like the Ink Spots and the rock and roll of Frankie Lymon and the Teenagers. This song was their first hit, and was written by their manager, Deborah Chessler.

The Chords, "Sh-Boom" (1954)
This song is a great example of why people started calling this style of rock and roll doo-wop. Listen to how the entire background of the song is made up of nonsense words—and the hook, "Sh-Boom!"

Little Anthony and the Imperials, "Tears on My Pillow" (1958)
"Little" Anthony Gourdine was given his nickname by DJ Alan Freed. Listen to Anthony's high falsetto voice that captured the attention of listeners everywhere but don't ignore the great background vocals by the Imperials.

LAB 7: THE BEATLES
INFLUENCED BY THE BEATLES
The Beatles had an enormous impact on the generations of musicians that came after them. A number of groups absorbed the Beatles' sound into their own music.

The Monkees, "I'm a Believer" (1966)
The Monkees started as a fictional Beatles-esque band on a U.S. television show. By 1967, they were an immensely popular group in their own right.

Badfinger, "Come and Get It" (1969)
It's not hard to hear the connection with Badfinger. They were signed to Apple Records (the one owned by the Beatles, not the computer company) and their early albums were produced by George Martin. This song was even written by Paul McCartney.

Electric Light Orchestra, "Mr. Blue Sky" (1977)
Jeff Lynne wanted his group to include orchestral instruments and push forward from where the Beatles left off. You can hear the Beatles' influence on Lynne in the string arrangements, piano parts, and vocal harmonies.

Oasis, "She's Electric" (1996)
While much of the Oasis album *(What's the Story) Morning Glory?* reveals the influence of the Beatles, this particular song is virtually a direct homage to the sound of the *White Album* (compare it to the song "While My Guitar Gently Weeps").

LAB 8: THE ROLLING STONES
INFLUENCED BY THE STONES
Like the Beatles, the Stones are one of the essential bands in rock history and many bands have been influenced by their music over the years.

The New York Dolls, "Personality Crisis" (1973)
The New York Dolls took the hard-rocking sound of the Stones and toughened it up with New York City attitude just a few years before the punk rock scene exploded. Great vocals from David Johansen (who later recorded a number of pop songs under the name Buster Poindexter).

Aerosmith, "Sweet Emotion" (1975)
Their rhythm and blues sound was spearheaded by lead singer Steven Tyler and guitarist Joe Perry, and it linked them to the Stones early on; but their 1975 album *Toys in the Attic* proved that they could take it somewhere new.

The Flamin' Groovies, "Shake Some Action" (1976)
When the Stones became popular in the United States in 1964, many bands in California attempted to replicate their sound. This is what I imagine the Stones would sound like if they were from San Francisco.

Guns and Roses, "Sympathy for the Devil" (1994)
This cover of the Rolling Stones song was recorded for the movie *Interview with a Vampire*. It is a pretty straightforward take on the original, but check out the blistering guitar solo by Slash.

LAB 9: THE SUPREMES
ALSO AT MOTOWN
Motown had a deep roster of artists during the 1960s and 1970s, and you should try to listen to as many of them as you can—but you can start by listening to these.

Barrett Strong, "Money (That's What I Want)" (1959)
This song was written by Berry Gordy and was the first hit record to come out of the Motown empire. It has been covered many times over the years by groups like the Beatles (1963) and the quirky new wave band the Flying Lizards (1979).

The Temptations, "My Girl" (1964)
Written by Roland White and Smokey Robinson, both of whom were members of the Miracles, this song was the Temptations' first number one hit. Listen to how the band (bass, guitar, and drums), the strings, and the voices all work to depict the emotion of the song.

Martha and the Vandellas, "Dancing in the Street" (1964)
A fun song about getting out and dancing in the streets during the summertime, but the song took on a deeper meaning when it was played as a part of civil rights demonstrations.

The Four Tops, "Reach Out (I'll Be There)" (1966)
This song perfectly showcases the elaborate arrangements made at Motown, from the opening flute melody and galloping wood blocks, to the powerful vocals and strings in the chorus.

LAB 10: JAMES BROWN
MORE MUSIC FROM KING RECORDS (1943–1968)
Take a listen to some of the varied musical artists who recorded at King Records over the years.

Bill Doggett, "Honky Tonk, Part 1 & 2" (1956)
Doggett was a great keyboard player and this instrumental track is sure to get everyone up and dancing. James Brown loved it so much, he recorded a super funky version with his band in 1972.

The Stanley Brothers, "Train 45" (1958)
The Stanley Brothers were one of the many country music acts to record for King. This song is an instrumental bluegrass tune with elaborate banjo picking.

Hank Ballard and the Midnighters, "The Twist" (1959)
You may know the more famous version of this song recorded a year later by Chubby Checker, but this one by Hank Ballard is the original.

Joe Tex, "Hold What You've Got" (1964)
Tex signed with King Records in 1955 and was often an opening act for James Brown. This song was his first big hit. I love the story he tells the listener in the middle (although it might be a bit too much for the younger kids listening).

LAB 11: BOB DYLAN
DYLAN LISTENED TO
Turn back the clock and listen to some of this American folk and rock and roll that influenced the young Bob Dylan.

Lead Belly, "Goodnight, Irene" (1933)
Huddie "Lead Belly" Ledbetter was a folk-blues musician who was famous for playing a twelve-string guitar. John Lomax, who was working for the Library of Congress, first recorded Lead Belly while he was in prison.

Woody Guthrie, "1913 Massacre" (1941)
Dylan's "Song for Woody" is based on the melody of this topical labor song that Guthrie wrote about the death of striking copper miners in 1913.

Pete Seeger, "If I Had a Hammer (The Hammer Song)" (1949)
Seeger is a great songwriter, banjo player, and political activist, and this song showcases the best of all of those. He also recorded a number of albums full of children's songs.

Little Richard, "Jenny, Jenny" (1957)
In his high school yearbook, Dylan wrote that he wanted to join Little Richard's band after graduation. Dylan played Little Richard songs like this one in his high school band. Little Richard recorded his original version at J&M Studios in New Orleans in 1957.

CHAPTER 2: ROCKING OUT
LAB 12: AFTER THE AIRPLANE
After the Airplane dissolved in 1972, many of the band members continued to work together in different combinations using variations of the band name.

Hot Tuna, "Hesitation Blues" (1970)
Hot Tuna was an acoustic-based folk-blues side project started by Jorma Kaukonen and Jack Casady in 1969, but it continued on after the end of the Airplane. This song is a traditional blues tune performed live by the band.

Jefferson Starship, "Miracles" (1975)
This song features many of the original Airplane members (such as Kantner, Slick, and Balin) but employs a pop-oriented sound. Listen for the beautiful string arrangement and vocal harmonies in the middle of the song.

Jefferson Starship, "Jane" (1979)
This song is from the album *Freedom at Point Zero*, and features new singer Mickey Thomas. It was a big move into a new arena rock sound, with a catchy rhythmic piano part and electric guitar solo.

Starship, "We Built This City" (1985)
With another new band name and an updated sound, you may not recognize this as some of the same musicians. The album *Knee Deep in the Hoopla* saw the return of Grace Slick, who sang dual lead vocals with Thomas.

LAB 13: THE BYRDS
MORE FOLK ROCK
By playing the music of Bob Dylan with a pop/rock instrumentation in 1965, the Byrds helped to launch the folk rock scene.

Simon and Garfunkel, "A Hazy Shade of Winter" (1966)
One of Simon and Garfunkel's most rocking songs, it owes a big debt to the Byrds' early folk rock. It is based on a gritty opening riff played by the acoustic guitar, while the lyrics ask the listener to look around and see the hazy shade of winter—a metaphor for the world as it existed in 1966.

Cat Stevens, "Wild World" (1970)
British singer-songwriter Cat Stevens had a folk rock hit with this song about a romantic breakup. Listen to how the voice, piano, guitar, and upright bass all work together in the opening of the song.

Crosby, Stills, Nash & Young, "Teach Your Children" (1970)
David Crosby's post-Byrds group performs this song with a powerful social message about how parents and children should always be learning from one another, but the vocal harmonies and steel pedal guitar (played by Jerry Garcia) are so beautiful that sometimes it's hard to pay attention to the words.

Joni Mitchell, "Big Yellow Taxi" (1970)
A folk rock classic that helped to draw attention to the growing environmental movement in the 1970s (in fact the organization Greenpeace formed between 1969 and 1972). I always enjoy the sweetness of her voice against the strummed acoustic guitar.

LAB 14: LED ZEPPELIN
MORE HARD ROCK SOUNDS
From the early 1970s forward, you can find many hard rock bands that took the power and energy of Led Zeppelin and made it their own. Here are just a few

Deep Purple, "Smoke on the Water" (1972)
Like Zeppelin, Deep Purple was there at the beginning of hard rock and heavy metal. This song features what might be one of the most recognizable guitar riff in all of classic rock.

AC/DC, "Back in Black" (1980)
This hard rock band formed in 1973 and has always been anchored by the sound of two brothers, Malcolm (bass) and Angus (guitar) Young. They have had the good fortune to work with two of the greatest hard rock singers—Bon Scott (in the early years) and Brian Johnson (since 1980). This song contains another essential hard rock guitar riff.

Van Halen, "Panama" (1984)
Another set of brothers forms the core of this band formed in 1972, Alex (drums and Eddie (guitar) Van Halen, and they have also worked with two amazing singers, David Lee Roth and Sammy Hagar. Eddie's guitar playing on this song rocks out, but it is also incredibly detailed—listen to all the little bends, squeaks and moans.

Them Crooked Vultures, "Mind Eraser, No Chaser" (2009)
A 2000s hard rock "supergroup" featuring ex-Zeppelin John Paul Jones with Dave Grohl (Nirvana, Foo Fighters) and Josh Homme (Queens of the Stone Age This song starts loud and never stops.

LAB 15: JIMI HENDRIX
Guitar Rock Sounds

Hendrix is often called one of the greatest rock guitarists to ever live, but that didn't stop some of these other greats from expanding on his sound and technique.

Stevie Ray Vaughan, "Voodoo Chile (Slight Return)" (1984)
Vaughn was already quite steeped in guitar history when he first heard "Purple Haze." The song inspired him to create his own rock guitar tone. This cover captures the essence of Hendrix's guitar sound as a tribute to it while simultaneously expanding on the musical techniques.

Joe Satriani, "Surfing with the Alien" (1987)
Satriani is an amazingly skilled electric guitar player. He was inspired to play the guitar after hearing a Hendrix song at the age of fourteen. He has also been an active teacher throughout his life and many of his students have gone on to fame.

Jennifer Batten, "Wanna Be Startin' Somethin'" (1992)
Batten first came into the spotlight as the guitarist for Michael Jackson from 1987 to 1997—she's the one in the videos with the big blonde hair. This version of Jackson's song appeared on her first solo album and all I can say is hold on to your hat!

Joe Bonamassa, "Blues Deluxe" (2003)
A blues-inspired player, Bonamassa found his passion in the sound of the British Invasion guitarists as is evidenced by this cover of the Jeff Beck Group. Make sure to listen to the killer solo that starts at four minutes.

LAB 16: YES
Progressive Sounds

Set aside an hour or two to listen to some of these great progressive rock epics.

King Crimson, "21st Century Schizoid Man" (1969)
Over the years, King Crimson has seen guitarist Robert Fripp collaborating with a rotating cast of musicians. This hard-rocking tune is the first song on their first album and features Greg Lake (who later joined Emerson, Lake & Palmer) singing with distortion added to his voice.

Genesis, "Watcher of the Skies" (1972)
Genesis was a pop rock powerhouse in the 1980s with drummer Phil Collins singing, but they began in 1967 as a progressive rock band with Peter Gabriel as the lead vocalist and primary songwriter. This song features a keyboard instrument called a Mellotron that was popular in the 1970s, and some impressive bass guitar playing by Mike Rutherford.

Emerson, Lake & Palmer, "Tarkus" (1971)
A 20-minute musical suite about an armadillo that is a giant living tank who battles a lizard/lobster/rocket launcher and a manticore, and then finally transforms into a peaceful ocean creature called "Aquatarkus." No . . . really. Luckily the music is awesome, especially if you like keyboard solos.

Rush, "2112" (1976)
A 20-minute sci-fi musical suite about a dystopian future in which the Priests of the Temples of Syrinx control the solar system and outlaw creativity, and the young boy who finds a guitar and writes his own songs to oppose them. A classic of prog rock and sci-fi! And let's not forget the awesome rocking music with outrageous drumming from Neil Peart.

LAB 17: PINK FLOYD
More from Outer Space

Set the controls for the heart of the Sun and get ready to rock out as these mind-blowing space rock tunes take you into the next dimension.

Soft Machine, "Moon in June" (1970)
An important band from the Canterbury music scene in England. This song is from the album *Third,* that saw them mixing psychedelic rock with jazz.

Hawkwind, "Master of the Universe" (1971)
From the band's second album, *In Search of Space,* a full-on science fiction–laced dose of space rock. The bass and drums set the tone with a motoric chugging rhythm that the other instruments can improvise over. Check out the wild sax solo in the middle.

Tangerine Dream, "Sunrise in the Third System" (1971)
Technically, the synthesizer-based group Tangerine Dream was part of a German musical movement in the late 1960s and early 1970s called Kosmiche Musik, but the name translates as Cosmic Music, and as such it fits right in here.

Can, "Future Days" (1973)
Another German Kosmiche Musik group, the band Can never achieved mainstream success, but they influenced countless other bands around the world. The persistent mellow groove of this song will have you dancing in a space trance in no time at all.

LAB 18: BLACK SABBATH
More Metal

If you like the music of Black Sabbath, then maybe you are a metal fan at heart, so go check out some of these other classic heavy metal tracks.

Ozzy Osbourne "Crazy Train" (1980)
After leaving Black Sabbath, Ozzy continued to have a very successful solo career where he further developed his character as the prince of darkness. "Crazy Train" from the album *Blizzard of Ozz* (1980) is one of his most famous songs and features the blistering guitar work of Randy Rhoads.

Iron Maiden, "The Number of the Beast" (1983)
Part of what was called the new wave of British heavy metal; Iron Maiden took the demonic elements of Black Sabbath and pushed it even further into the realm of horror films. This song is actually about the terror of witnessing a meeting of witches (so not great for young kids), but it contains one of the best rock screams ever at 1:18 produced by lead singer Bruce Dickinson.

Poison, "Nothin' but a Good Time" (1988)
If all this doom and gloom is too much for you, then maybe the Glam/Hair metal sound of bands like Poison is more your speed. This is a fun song about working 9 to 5 at a job you might hate, but letting loose with your friends at the end of the day is what really matters.

Metallica, "Enter Sandman" (1991)
Originally a thrash metal band from LA, this group went on to superstardom with their self-titled album in 1991 (often called the black album by fans). This song is about nightmares and bad dreams—not a good idea to play it before bed.

LAB 19: CREAM
CLAPTON BEFORE AND AFTER CREAM

Eric Clapton is one of rock and roll's great guitarists, and he played with a number of bands over the years.

The Yardbirds, "For Your Love" (1965)
This song may be the most famous by Clapton's first band the Yardbirds, but it is also the song that signaled his departure. Clapton thought the sound was too pop with not enough blues influence.

Blind Faith, "Can't Find My Way Home" (1969)
Another supergroup featuring Clapton and Ginger Baker (Cream) along with Steve Winwood (Traffic) and Ric Grech (Family). Winwood's sweet vocals soar over Clapton's plucked acoustic guitar.

Derek and the Dominos, "Layla" (1970)
Clapton's attempt to be part of a band that was not a supergroup—it didn't help that guitarist Duane Allman of the Allman Brothers became involved! The piano and guitar finale actually takes up the entire second half of the song.

Eric Clapton, "Tears In Heaven" (1992)
Clapton showed that he could still write and record a great pop song when he wrote this emotional tune inspired by the death of his four-year-old son.

CHAPTER 3: DEEP SOUL
LAB 20: RAY CHARLES
RHYTHM AND BLUES

Ray Charles started as an R&B artist, so let's take a listen to some more great R&B sounds from the 1950s.

Johnny Otis, "Double Crossing Blues" (1950)
Based in Los Angeles, Otis was considered to be the godfather of rhythm and blues. In addition to recording his own music, he also discovered and produced a number of artists including Etta James, Big Jay McNeely, and Little Esther (who sings on this song).

Lloyd Price, "Lawdy Miss Clawdy" (1952)
This song was written by Lloyd Price and recorded at J&M Studios in New Orleans. It features performances by Fats Domino, Dave Bartholomew, and Earl Palmer.

Bo Diddley, "Bo Diddley" (1955)
Recorded at Chess Records in Chicago, this tune features an important rhythm that Diddley became famous for, called the clave rhythm (which he took from Afro-Cuban music). Try to count along with the pulse that goes, 1 – 2 – 3, 1 – 2. It's a very infectious rhythm!

Sam Cooke, "Chain Gang" (1960)
Cooke started as a gospel singer and then began to sing R&B and soul in the 1950s. This song was one of his early hits. I love the sound of the metal hammers used as percussion (to re-create the sound of the workers on the chain gang).

LAB 21: SOLOMON BURKE
MORE R&B AND SOUL SOUNDS FROM ATLANTIC RECORDS

Burke was excited to walk through the doors of Atlantic Records in 1960 because so many great artists had recorded there in the 1950s. Here are just a few to get you started:

The Drifters, "Money Honey" (1953)
This group was founded by singer Clyde McPhatter in 1953, and "Money Honey" was their first hit for Atlantic Records. Listen to the backing vocals and the fantastic saxophone part.

Ruth Brown, "Mama, He Treats Your Daughter Mean" (1953)
Ruth Brown was such a success during the early days of Atlantic Records that they actually started calling the label "the house that Ruth built." Listen to how she cracks her voice to add emotion to the cries for her mama.

Big Joe Turner, "Flip, Flop, and Fly" (1955)
Big Joe was known as a Kansas City Shouter for his powerful vocal style. This song was the follow-up to his 1954 hit "Shake, Rattle, and Roll," and both were mainstays in the early days of rock and roll.

The Coasters, "Yakety Yak" (1958)
If you have young kids, this song is a riot to listen to and sing along with because of its use of nonsense words, the changes in vocal register, and the silly story. This was recorded in 1958, but would we call it rock and roll or rhythm and blues?

LAB 22: ARETHA FRANKLIN
Take 'em to Church
Like many of her soul music contemporaries, Aretha got her start by listening to and performing gospel music. Here are some of the artists she was listening to

The Dixie Hummingbirds, "Amazing Grace" (1946)
Formed in 1928, this group was known for their energetic stage shows and vocal harmony. Their syncopated vocal technique is on display in this recording from 1946.

The Blind Boys of Alabama,
"I Can See Everybody's Mother but Mine" (1948)
This is the first song recorded by this group, whose name tells you a lot about them. Believe it or not, a version of the group is still recording and touring today.

The Soul Stirrers, "Jesus Gave Me Water" (1951)
This group formed in the early 1930s and was a major force in popularizing the sound of modern gospel music. Sam Cooke was the group's lead singer at the time of this recording.

Mahalia Jackson, "Take My Hand, Precious Lord" (1956)
Jackson was known as the Queen of Gospel and was one of the most influential gospel singers of all time. She worked frequently with Thomas A. Dorsey (the Father of Gospel Music), who wrote this song, which she sang at Dr. Martin Luther King Jr.'s funeral in 1968.

LAB 23: WILSON PICKETT
Originally Recorded By
Check out the original versions of some of these songs made famous by Wilson Pickett and compare what you hear. How did he change the song? What stayed the same?

Sir Mack Rice, "Mustang Sally" (1965)
A classic soul song played by bands in bars all over the United States. Pickett made it famous, but check out this version by the guy who wrote the song.

Cannibal & the Headhunters, "Land of 1,000 Dances" (1965)
This band was part of the LA garage rock scene, and even made a video for this song. This version has the same melody but is missing the "feel" of the Pickett version.

Dyke & the Blazers, "Funky Broadway" (1967)
There is still a great groove on this original record, but Pickett's voice really brings the melody alive in his version.

LAB 24: MARVIN GAYE
Soul into the 1970s
Soul music in the 1970s evolved as musicians used new sounds and sang about many of the continued struggles of life in the United States for African Americans.

Curtis Mayfield, "Move on Up" (1971)
A song with a great hook and a percussion-heavy groove that sets out a positive message of self-affirmation—and although he never actually says it directly in the lyrics, the song contained an important message of black pride for the 1970s.

Al Green, "Let's Stay Together" (1972)
During the 1970s, Green recorded a series of hit records at Hi Records in Memphis with producer Willie Mitchell. Listen to how soft and breathy Green's voice is in the recording and the galloping rhythm of the drums.

Stevie Wonder, "Living for the City" (1973)
This song starts with Wonder playing the digital piano along with a thumping synthesizer bass. The lyrics paint a dramatic picture of the post–civil rights era struggles of African Americans in the United States.

The O'Jays, "For the Love of Money" (1973)
The O'Jays were from Canton, Ohio, but they became famous as part of the Philly Soul sound. This song was written by the team of Kenny Gamble and Leon Huff and features a soul funk groove. And by the way, if you listen closely you'll find out that the love of money is not such a good thing.

LAB 25: THE STAPLE SINGERS
Sounds out of Stax
Take a listen to some of these great artists who recorded for Stax:

Booker T. & the M.G.'s, "Green Onions" (1962)
This band was made up of members of the Stax Records house band. While their playing can be heard on hundreds of records, they were really able to stretch out on their own recordings. This is the first song on their first album.

Otis Redding, "Mr. Pitiful" (1964)
One of the early talents of Stax Records, Redding died at the height of his career in a 1967 plane crash. This song jumps and grooves, and if you want to hear some of the best horn sections that soul music has to offer, then you came to the right place.

William Bell, "I Forgot to Be Your Lover" (1968)
There are more popular songs by this Memphis-born singer and songwriter, but for me, this song perfectly represents the sweet soul sound. His voice floats over the strings, bass, drums, and electric guitar, but if we listen closely we can hear strong emotions that he expresses with his voice.

Isaac Hayes, "Walk on By" (1969)
Hayes was one of the major forces behind the development of the Southern soul sound created at Stax in the late 1960s. The dramatic nature of this song is almost too much to take: his powerful voice, the backing singers, the string and horn arrangements, and that great fuzz tone guitar!

CHAPTER 4: PUNK ROCK

LAB 26: THE RAMONES
ALSO APPEARING AT CBGB'S

A number of other famous bands got their start at CBGBs, and even though they all sounded quite different, they each felt connected to the growing punk movement.

Television, "Marquee Moon" (1977)
Television was one of the key bands on the New York City club scene in the mid-1970s, and they were one of the first bands to play at CBGBs on a regular basis. The song "Marquee Moon" is a cult classic, and it shows how the early Punk rock sound in NYC was quite diverse. The sound of Television was defined by lead guitarist, Tom Verlaine.

The Dead Boys, "Sonic Reducer" (1977)
Originally from Cleveland, Ohio, they made their mark in the early CBGBs punk scene—and they probably have the most recognizably punk sound of the early bands. Stiv Bators raw vocal shouts over the sonic blast of guitarists Cheetah Chrome and Jimmy Zero—classic punk!

Suicide, "Ghost Rider" (1977)
Don't let the name scare you away from listing to this group, which is actually a duo from New York consisting of Alan Vega (vocals) and Martin Rev (synthesizers). If you thought all punk was just guitars and shouting vocals, then Suicide might change your mind. They made punk music with synthesizers and influenced many musicians to come, even if they never found mainstream success themselves.

Richard Hell and the Voidoids, "Blank Generation" (1976)
Hell started as a member of Television, but soon split to go his own way and perform a rougher style of rock. This song is often seen as one of the first to actually define the punk scene in NYC as lost souls, giving them the name the "Blank Generation" in reference to the 1959 song "The Beat Generation."

LAB 27: THE CLASH
MORE BRITISH PUNK

Spike up your hair in a Mohawk, put on some Doc Martens boots and black eyeliner, and get ready to rock with the best of British punk rock.

The Damned, "New Rose" (1976)
Much like the Ramones in the United States, you can hear the Damned's love for classic rock and roll in their music. The opening dialogue, "Is she really going out with him" is a reference to the Shangri-Las 1965 hit "Leader of the Pack."

Sex Pistols, "God Save the Queen" (1977)
The Pistols were the first band to take the New York City punk rock sound and connect it to the political landscape of England in the 1970s. It's not hard to figure out what they're talking about when singer Johnny Rotten calls the Queen of England's rule a "fascist regime" in the first line of the song.

Generation X, "Dancing with Myself" (1980)
One of the early British punk bands, Generation X is also famous for launching the career of singer Billy Idol. He rerecorded this song during his solo career, but this is the original that features more distorted punk rock guitar.

Siouxsie and the Banshees, "Christine" (1980)
This group formed from members of the punk rock scene that hung out with the Sex Pistols. Lead singer Siouxsie Sioux was known for her innovations in punk fashion and her songwriting. The band's music pushed punk into a more experimental area that eventually became the postpunk sound.

LAB 28: PATTI SMITH
INFLUENCED BY SMITH

Smith was influenced by musicians like Bob Dylan, David Bowie, and The Stooges. Here are some artists who were influenced by Smith.

The Pretenders, "My City Was Gone" (1982)
The Pretenders were formed by singer/songwriter/guitarist Chrissie Hynde as a punk band, and I think you can hear a bit of Smith in her vocal style. This song is about her return to Akron, Ohio, after years away only to find the city had suffered the effects of a severe economic decline.

The Breeders, "Cannonball" (1993)
The sound of this song was unique when it came out in 1993. The verse is propelled forward by Kim Deal's catchy bass line, and the song explodes into a fierce chorus.

Hole, "Doll Parts" (1994)
Featuring lead singer Courtney Love, this group was known for their aggressive sound and feminist lyrics. Listen to how the energy of this song ebbs and flows as it repeats the same three chords over and over.

LAB 29: TALKING HEADS
Punk Rock/Art Rock Mix-ups

The Talking Heads' version of punk was influenced by the art music scene in New York City. Here are some other bands who mixed punk power and art rock style:

The Velvet Underground, "I Heard Her Call My Name" (1968)
The original art rock/protopunk New York City band. They even had famed artist Andy Warhol as their manager! It has a melody and you can sing along, if you can hear the words over the blasting guitar.

Gang of Four, "Damaged Goods" (1978)
A British band that, much like the Clash and the Talking Heads, looked to expand the sound of punk by bringing in additional musical influences. The brittle guitar adds the perfect sound for this dark breakup song.

Radiohead, "Packt Like Sardines in a Crushed Tin Box" (2000)
I don't think a lot of people know that this band takes its name from a Talking Heads song, "Radio Head" (1986). This song shows their experimentation with new sounds and electronics.

Arcade Fire, "Reflektor" (2013)
When I listen to this indie rock band from Montreal, Canada, it always makes me think of the Talking Heads. They both have an affinity for world music rhythms and a similar sense of melody.

LAB 30: THE REPLACEMENTS
American Heartland Punk Rock

Here are some more postpunk sounds from across the United States:

They Might Be Giants, "We Are the Replacements" (1987)
This song is an homage to the Replacements that expands on the original joke of how that band got its name—audiences were expecting to see a different band and got only the replacement band. I love the old rock and roll organ!

Social Distortion, "Ball and Chain" (1990)
Out of Orange County, California, this band represents the thriving West Coast punk scene. Social "D" (as they are often called) were inspired by a mix of the Rolling Stones, Johnny Cash, and the Clash. And guess what? I think you can hear all of that in their music.

The Goo Goo Dolls, "We Are the Normal" (1993)
From Buffalo, New York, they rose from the underground punk scene to become one of the major alternative rock bands of the late twentieth century. This song was cowritten by one of their heroes—Paul Westerberg.

The Gaslight Anthem, "Angry Johnny and the Radio" (2007)
This New Jersey band is often described as a mix of punk and Bruce Springsteen. I can see that . . . and this song really shows how much their version of punk is rooted in the Replacements.

CHAPTER 5: DANCE MUSIC
LAB 31: MICHAEL JACKSON
Influenced by the King of Pop

To say that Michael Jackson influenced other musicians is like saying the sky is blue. Here's just a small selection of musicians who wear their love for Jackson on their sleeves:

Justin Timberlake, "Like I Love You" (2002)
Everything about this tune sounds like Michael. The whispered introduction, the low-key verse voices with a touch of rasp in his voice, and the high falsetto vocal in the chorus. The backing track even sounds like '90s Jackson.

Usher, "There Goes My Baby" (2010)
There are a lot of Usher songs that draw musical inspiration from Michael Jackson, but personally, I like this one because it shows a connection to Jackson's slow songs like "You Are Not Alone."

Chris Brown, "She Ain't You" (2011)
While Chris Brown frequently invokes Jackson's sound, this song is interesting because it actually samples the song "Human Nature." First, the music uses Jackson's song, and then it transitions to a reproduction of the music using newer synthesizers. Even Brown's melody is an approximation of Jackson's.

Alien Ant Farm, "Smooth Criminal" (2001)
This rock band recorded a direct Michael Jackson cover, and while it might be hard to say that the rest of their songs were influenced by Jackson, it is amazing how well this song translates from the sound of the original dance epic into an aggressive rock performance.

LAB 32: EARTH, WIND & FIRE
Funky Big Bands

Get ready to dance with some of these classic tunes from large bands with funky horn sections.

Kool and the Gang, "Hollywood Swinging" (1974)
This song features a lot of musicians all falling into the groove to create something with an irresistible dance sound. "Hollywood Swinging" has also been sampled in numerous hip hop songs, such as in "Feel So Good" by Mase (1997).

Average White Band, "Pick Up the Pieces" (1974)
The Average White Band is a bunch of white guys who play funk and R&B and are from Scotland. No . . . you heard me right . . . from Scotland. Say what you want, but that horn section doesn't lie.

The Ohio Players, "Love Rollercoaster" (1976)
This band hails from Dayton, Ohio, and features a fantastic rhythm section and horns. The song uses the idea of a roller coaster to talk about the ups and downs of a relationship. Did I mention the horns?

Commodores, "Brick House" (1977)
A funky soul band that also knew how to record mellow ballads and featured Lionel Richie as one of the original lead singers. This song features lead vocals by drummer William King.

LAB 33: CHIC
ON THE ROAD TO DISCO AND BEYOND
Let's take a listen to the influence of Edwards and Rodgers on the music of the late '70s and early '80s.

Peaches & Herb, "Shake Your Groove Thing" (1978)
This group feature Herb Fame (the Herb) and Francine Barker (the Peaches). This song was produced by Freddie Perren and is anchored by a memorable melodic bass line and a large band arrangement.

Sister Sledge, "We Are Family" (1979)
This song was written and produced by Edwards and Rodgers and performed by the female vocal group Sister Sledge from Philadelphia. This song is a mix of disco and R&B elements.

The Sugarhill Gang, "Rapper's Delight" (1979)
I had to include this example here because this might be one of the most famous examples of hip hop DJs taking a record and using it to make their own music. Take a listen. The entire backing track of "Rapper's Delight" is based on the groove of the break section from "Good Times."

Diana Ross, "I'm Coming Out" (1980)
Another song written and produced by Rodgers and Edwards. The song's lyrics made sense to Ross, who was leaving Motown and taking more control of her career, but Rodgers originally got the idea from seeing how many drag queens in NYC performed dressed as Ross. As such, it has been a key song to express pride within the LGBT community over the years.

LAB 34: DONNA SUMMER
MORE DISCO DIVAS
Here are some other top female singers of the disco era

Vicki Sue Robinson, "Turn the Beat Around" (1976)
An early disco-era hit, this song established key elements in the disco sound including the auxiliary percussion (congas, shakers, etc.), full arrangements featuring horns and strings, and the vocal gymnastics of the female vocal lead.

Anita Ward, "Ring My Bell" (1979)
This song was Anita Ward's only major success, but the song has become a classic of the disco era and continues to be covered and sampled today.

Gloria Gaynor, "I Will Survive" (1979)
This song features a musical structure common in many disco songs sung by women—a slow start where the singer tells a story and then a fast-paced song with a full disco arrangement.

Cher, "Bad Love" (1980)
Cher started as a backup singer in the early 1960s and went on to be an international superstar, even hosting her own television show for years. This song comes from her 1980 album produced by Giorgio Moroder.

LAB 35: THE BEE GEES
EVERYONE BOOGIE DOWN
The backlash against disco that happened at the end of the 1970s often makes many people forget that a number of more traditional rock artists also recorded their own hit disco songs in the wake of the Bee Gees' success.

The Rolling Stones, "Miss You" (1978)
Mick Jagger was a regular at the Studio 54 disco and was enamored by the sound of black dance music all his life. In 1978, the Rolling Stones put forth their own rock version of disco that even produced their first 12-inch single. The bass line by Bill Wyman is marvelous.

Rod Stewart, "Do Ya Think I'm Sexy?" (1978)
Stewart was well known for his British blues-rock sound with the Jeff Beck Group and the Faces, but this song from his solo career dove full-on into disco territory. The music features the classic bass and drums of disco and even highlights a synthesizer and string melody in the postchorus.

Kiss, "I Was Made for Lovin' You" (1979)
The rhythm section plays a spot-on disco rhythm, but the distorted electric guitars keep one foot in the rock world. As an interesting side note, Kiss was signed to Casablanca Records, the home to Donna Summer and the Village People.

Paul McCartney and Wings, "Goodnight Tonight" (1979)
Disco music even influenced the former Beatle Paul McCartney to write this song for his new group Wings. Check out that rhythm section with a funky bass part played by Paul.

LAB 36: MADONNA
STRIKE A POSE
Many of the successful women on the pop charts today owe a great debt to Madonna. Here are just a few

Christina Aguilera, "What a Girl Wants" (1999)
Aguilera's more recent music may not sound like it's influenced by Madonna, but in this early song, the connection is obvious. We can also see a clear connection to Madonna's strong personality and her ability to reinvent herself.

Britney Spears, "Me Against the Music" (2003)
Spears has always talked about the influence Madonna had on her music and dance, and in 2003 the two got to work together on this song. Not necessarily the best song from either of them, in my opinion, but the combination of the two made it a big hit.

Katy Perry, "Teenage Dream" (2010)
Perry has taken Madonna's pop music template and turned it into a twenty-first-century powerhouse. Her string of hit songs, films, and videos seems to have no end. The music of this song is very catchy and the chorus feels like it is going to break out of the speakers and jump into the room.

Lady Gaga, "Born This Way" (2011)
Lady Gaga's shifting stage persona shows her interest in Madonna, and this song is an almost direct remake, or maybe I should say reimagining, of Madonna's "Express Yourself."

CHAPTER 6: NEW ROCK SOUNDS
LAB 37: PARLIAMENT-FUNKADELIC
FROM THE MINDS OF THE P-FUNK
Take a listen to some more music created by members of P-Funk.

The Parliaments, "Time" (1968)
This is not funk, but it is fun to hear the music of George Clinton's first group (from which the Parliament name comes). Clinton said he wanted the group to be an updated version of Frankie Lymon and the Teenagers. See if you can hear the sound of soul and doo-wop in the music.

Bootsy's Rubber Band, "I'd Rather Be with You" (1976)
This group was a side project for P-Funk led by bass player Bootsy Collins, and this song comes from their first album. It features a haunting melody and a pulsing bass line from Bootsy.

Eddie Hazel, "California Dreamin'" (1977)
This song, from guitarist Eddie Hazel's only solo record, *Game, Dames and Guitar Thangs*, is a cover of the tune by the Mamas & the Papas. It serves as a perfect showcase for Eddie's scorching and trippy guitar playing. Listen closely to the solo in the middle.

George Clinton, "Atomic Dog" (1982)
This song comes from the 1982 album *Computer Games*, which is technically Clinton's first solo album although all the music is performed by the P-Funk players. It features the famous lyric "bow-wow-woww-yippie-yo-yippie-yeah" —a line that has been sampled in many hip hop songs.

LAB 38: QUEEN
GLAM ROCK–ZEALOUS SOUNDS
Glam rock was one of many styles that influenced the music of Queen. Take a listen to some of the other bands who played this melodic style of hard rock.

T Rex, "Bang a Gong (Get It On)" (1971)
Written by lead singer Marc Bolan, this song has a prominent guitar hook and a memorable singalong chorus. Listen to how the chorus builds up the musical texture by adding voices, strings, and drumbeat.

Gary Glitter, "Rock and roll Part 1 & 2" (1972)
The world of professional sports has made sure that anyone who has ever attended a major sporting event knows the "part 2" of this song—it's a common sing-along. But the original song was two parts on the A and B sides of a 45 rpm record. The point of this song? You guessed it—rock and roll!

Mott the Hoople, "All the Young Dudes" (1972)
This song is from the 1972 album of the same name that was produced by David Bowie. When I was , I used to think it was recorded by the Beatles. Can you guess why? What do you hear in the music?

Sweet, "Ballroom Blitz" (1973)
This song is a staple of FM rock radio, but many people still don't know who recorded it. The music features an upfront drum part that plays a shuffle rhythm as the electric guitars play the main riff. The song goes back and forth between the mellow verses and the all out "blitz" of the vocal-heavy chorus.

LAB 39: JOURNEY
THE SOUNDS OF ARENA ROCK
These bands perfected a big rock sound with lots of melodic hooks that worked well in a large stadium show—but the records also sounded pretty good in your bedroom or in a video arcade while playing Pong.

Boston, "More Than a Feeling" (1976)
Two things make this song great. One, the "never get tired of this" guitar riff played by Tom Scholz, and two, the amazing multitracked vocal parts all sung by Brad Delp. Note to listeners: Play this loud, preferably while in the car.

Styx, "Come Sail Away" (1977)
Some of you might want to argue about which Styx song is the best one to mention here, but I love this one because it shows all the musical sides of the band. The power ballad piano opening, the hard-rocking middle section, the spacey synthesizer bridge, and the final full-on arena rock ending.

Foreigner, "Cold as Ice" (1977)
The piano establishes the swagger of the song until the full band enters to rock this one out—it even has a synthesizer break and a guitar solo! The groove makes you want to join in, especially when the great background vocals enter.

REO Speedwagon, "Take It on the Run" (1981)
By the early 1980s, the sound of arena rock began to mellow from its hard rock roots and focus more on the ballad side of the songs. "Take It on the Run" starts with an acoustic folk rock sound before the electric guitars enter to add a bit more rock into the mix. Listen to the great harmonies sung by the band members and the guitar solo by Gary Richrath (who also wrote the song).

LAB 40: HEART
WOMEN WHO ROCK
In the late 1970s Heart really set the path for a number of female artists to break into the mainstream during the early 1980s.

Pat Benatar, "Hit Me with Your Best Shot" (1979)
Benatar grew up on Long Island, New York, and did most of her early performing in musical theater. When she finally began to sing rock and roll, she found a powerful voice that captured pop music audiences.

Joan Jett & the Blackhearts, "I Love Rock 'n' Roll" (1981)
Jett began her musical career as a rhythm guitarist and singer in the band the Runaways. This song is a cover of a song by Arrows—but Jett's version is now the absolute definitive one. Just listen to the attitude she sings with—it's punk and rock all mixed up into one.

The Go-Go's, "We Got the Beat" (1982)
Formed in 1978, The Go-Go's wrote their own songs, played their own instruments, and pushed against many of the preconceptions about women in rock and roll. Their unique sound in songs like this helped to create the sound of new wave rock in the 1980s.

The Bangles, "In a Different Light" (1985)
I know that the Bangles have had much bigger pop hits, but this great song written by band members Susanna Hoffs and Vicki Peterson shows just how much they could rock.

LAB 41: FLEETWOOD MAC
SOFT ROCK SEVENTIES SOUNDS
If there is hard rock, then there has to be soft rock. These bands often draw from country or jazz influences and don't have the same aggressive nature of their hard rock brethren. Many of these songs helped to create the "adult contemporary" radio format in the 1970s.

Eagles, "Take It Easy" (1972)
Based in Los Angeles, the Eagles perfected a form of country rock while working with legendary producer Glyn Johns. Listen carefully for all the guitar parts in the music, and some great banjo picking by Bernie Leadon. A big part of their sound came from their distinct ability to sing complex vocal harmony.

Steely Dan, "Rikki Don't Lose That Number" (1974)
Walter Becker and Donald Fagen got their start working in the Brill Building and then created the jazz-influenced band, Steely Dan. Listen to how the music allows for each instrument to have its own space as a part of the soundscape. These guys know how to write a great melody.

Dire Straits, "Sultans of Swing" (1978)
This was the first single released by pub rock band Dire Straits and was written by lead guitarist and vocalist Mark Knopfler. It tells a story about a jazz band called the Sultans of Swing playing in small clubs around London. Listen to how the main vocal and guitar play in call and response throughout the song.

Christopher Cross, "Ride Like the Wind" (1979)
I love everything about this song. The fake wind in the introduction. The held-out piano chords and synthesizer tones. The string arrangement in the background with the conga drums. The fact that Michael McDonald from the Doobie Brothers sings backup is just icing on the cake.

LAB 42: HALL & OATES
BLUE-EYED SOULFUL SOFT ROCK SEVENTIES SOUNDS
Here are some great soft rock artists who have been given the label blue-eyed soul over the years:

Ace, "How Long" (1974)
Lead singer Paul Carrack wrote this song about the bass player of Ace when Carrack found out he was recording with other musicians (the chorus says "how long has this been going on"). The down tempo song features some amazing vocal harmonies in the chorus.

Ambrosia, "How Much I Feel" (1978)
This group had a series of hit songs in the late 1970s, but this one written by lead singer and guitarist David Pack is their most popular by far. Listen to how smooth all the voices fit together in the chorus.

The Doobie Brothers, "What a Fool Believes" (1979)
Written by lead singer Michael McDonald and his friend Kenny Loggins, listen to how McDonald's voice slurs the words, rises up to high falsetto notes, and then back down to low ones in his natural voice.

Steve Winwood, "While You See a Chance" (1980)
Winwood was an amazing musician from a very early age and played in a number of bands before recording his first solo album. On this record, he played every single instrument by himself. And as a side note—in my opinion, the entire album *Arc of a Diver* might be one of the most perfect albums ever recorded.

LAB 43: BRUCE SPRINGSTEEN
'70S ROCK SINGER/SONGWRITERS

There were a number of talented male singer-songwriters who all got their start in the 1970s, and most of them played either piano or guitar as they sang their songs.

Billy Joel, "Scenes from an Italian Restaurant" (1977)
From Long Island, New York, Billy Joel sang songs that were about everyday people and their problems in life—and by the success of his music, it appears that many listeners were able to relate. This song tells a great story as the music moves through several different sections.

Elton John, "Candle in the Wind" (1974/1997)
This song was originally written by John and his songwriting partner Bernie Taupin as a tribute to Marilyn Monroe, but when they changed the lyrics to lament the death of Princess Diana of Wales in 1997, it became the second highest selling single of all time.

John Mellencamp, "Small Town" (1985)
Mellencamp is known as the voice of the heartland, and this song is a tribute to all the small towns across the United States. He himself was from a small town in Indiana.

Bob Seger, "Mainstreet" (1977)
Seger recorded this song with the famous Muscle Shoals Rhythm Section. The lyrics reference Main Street, an all-American symbol, but Seeger is also talking about one in particular in Ann Arbor, Michigan.

LAB 44: KISS
MAKEUP AND THEATRICAL STAGE SHOWS

Here are a few rock and heavy metal bands that have used makeup and presented their band members as characters over the years. Warning: Most of this is not for little kids.

Alice Cooper, "Welcome to My Nightmare" (1975)
The band Alice Cooper established itself as the antihippie rock band in the late 1960s. Inspired by horror films, their stage show included snakes, fake blood, monsters, and lighting effects. The same horror-based theme came out in songs like this one (which they performed on *The Muppet Show*).

Gwar, "Sick of You" (1990)
This band was formed by a bunch of students at Virginia Commonwealth University who mixed their love of heavy metal, science fiction, and horror movies with elaborate costumes and performance art. Their live shows are crazy and sometimes quite gross.

Mr. Bungle, "None of Them Knew They Were Robots" (1998)
A great experimental music band that includes Mike Patton (who became

famous as the lead singer for Faith No More) and, like all the other bands on this list, performed live wearing masks. I love the way this song cycles through a ton of musical styles over the 6 minutes, almost like the music was wearing a mask.

Slipknot, "Before I Forget" (2005)
This band always presents themselves in masks and costume and, musically, they are a great example of post-1990s metal that features a rap music element.

CHAPTER 7: NEW WAVE
LAB 45: ROXY MUSIC
THE NEW ROMANTICS

Beginning in the late 1970s in England, an entire musical scene developed that tried to capture the sound, look, and feel of Roxy Music, called the new romantics.

Japan, "Suburban Love" (1978)
The band Japan is one of my personal favorites, and while they always claimed that they were not actually part of the new romantic movement in England, they were still one of the best examples of it. This is a love song for the suburban sprawl of the modern era (of the late 1970s, that is).

Duran Duran, "Union of the Snake" (1983)
Duran Duran became a never-ending hit machine in the 1980s, and much of their musical sound came from their love of Roxy Music and Japan—just listen to the vocal sound and the bass lines. This song was the lead single from their third album *Seven and the Ragged Tiger*.

Ultravox, "Vienna" (1981)
The sound of Ultravox was somewhere between new wave rock and full-on synth-pop, and it featured a vocal sound and melodies sung by Midge Ure that were a clear connection to Roxy Music.

ABC, "The Look of Love (Part 1)" (1982)
This song is from the band's first album that was produced by Trevor Horn and arranged by Anne Dudley and JJ Jeczalik of the band the Art of Noise. You can hear the ultramodern soul-chic of Roxy Music right away. The original single featured four "parts," or versions, but part 1 is the most famous.

LAB 46: BLONDIE
HIP HOP SOUNDS

While Blondie was making music in downtown New York City at clubs like CBGB, a musical revolution was taking place in the Bronx. Here are some of the early hit records to come out of hip hop:

Fatback Band, "King Tim III (Personality Jock)" (1979)
This group was a successful funk/disco band in the late 1970s that was famous for their song the "Spanish Hustle." But when vocalist Tim Washington added a rap to this song in 1979, it became one of the first recorded examples of hip hop music.

Funky 4 + 1, "That's the Joint" (1980)
One of the first hip hop groups in the Bronx to sign a record deal and one of the first to feature the skills of a female MC in the form of Sha Rock. Listen for the way this song uses a musical break from the song "Rescue Me" by A Taste of Honey.

Grandmaster Flash and the Furious Five, "The Message" (1982)
Grandmaster Flash was one of the first superstar DJs in hip hop culture, and this song was one of the first socially conscious rap songs to reach a level of mainstream success. Listen to the sound of the backing tracks and the emotion in MC Melle Mel's voice.

Afrika Bambaataa & the Soul Sonic Force, "Planet Rock" (1982)
For this song, DJ Afrika Bambaataa (another pioneer of hip hop DJing) used a number of records by the German synthesizer band Kraftwerk to create one of the funkiest backing tracks in all of old-school hip hop.

LAB 47: DAVID BOWIE
New Wave Rock

The list of musicians influenced by David Bowie is long and diverse, so let's focus on new wave musicians from the 1980s that owe him a debt of gratitude.

Adam Ant, "Goody Two Shoes" (1982)
Adam Ant was the lead singer of the new romantic group Adam and the Ants, and he gained a lot of inspiration from Bowie's music. This song is from Ant's first solo album. Listen closely to see if you can hear how the Bowie-inspired glam rock elements mix with new wave sounds.

INXS, "Original Sin" (1983)
Although this moody and catchy song appeared on the fourth album by Australian rock band INXS, it was their first official single, produced by Nile Rodgers. Can you hear some sonic similarities to Bowie's "Let's Dance"?

The Police, "Every Breath You Take" (1983)
When the album Synchronicity came out in 1983, many critics compared lead singer Sting to Bowie, both in terms of the band's musical adeptness and the way that Sting had become a full-on British pop star who also courted a darker artistic muse. This song is so catchy, but the lyrics . . . so dark.

The Cars, "Heartbeat City" (1984)
The Cars were a band out of Boston who mixed guitar rock with synthesizers to create their own new wave sound. The stark sound of their music and the sleek voice of lead singer Ric Ocasek often remind me of Bowie.

LAB 48: DEVO
New Wave Experimentalism

The idea of experimentalism in new wave could take many forms. Some musicians pushed for completely new sounds, and others looked back to the past with a sense of camp and irony. Take a listen to some of these bands and see what you think was experimental about each of them.

Pere Ubu, "The Modern Dance" (1978)
This band came out of Cleveland, Ohio, during the punk music era, but they were greatly influenced by the fact that they lived in an industrial city. Listen to the hammers and steam pumps in the background and to how intense and nervous lead singer David Thomas sounds as he sings.

The B-52s, "Rock Lobster" (1979)
The B-52s took their name from a World War II bomber, wore beehive hairdos and bright-colored clothing, and sang songs like "Rock Lobster"—a song about a rock and roll beach party with marine animals. The surf guitar riff and cheesy organ sounds really make it for me.

Sparks, "Rock and Roll People in a Disco World" (1980)
This song comes from an album produced by Euro disco legends Giorgio Moroder and Harold Faltermeyer (Faltermeyer wrote the popular '80s instrumental "Axel F"). This song contains a mixture of rock and disco sounds, but the band is also poking fun at themselves as a former rock band who had been seduced by the sound of synthesizers and disco.

Nine Inch Nails, "Head Like a Hole" (1989)
Like Devo and Pere Ubu, this band got its start in northeast Ohio making modern industrial dance music with a focus on synthesizers. The mainstream success of the album Pretty Hate Machine influenced numerous bands that were suddenly looking to capture the pop-industrial sound.

LAB 49: DEPECHE MODE
Synth-Pop Sounds

The mid- to late 1980s saw an explosion of synth-pop bands in England and the United States. Here are several bands that went on to make substantial contributions to the history of the style:

The Human League, "Don't You Want Me" (1983)
The Human League began as an experimental electronic band, and in 1983 lead singer Philip Oakey pushed them toward a pop music sound rooted in synthesizers and filled with melodic hooks. This song was the first true hit song of the synth-pop musical style.

New Order, "Blue Monday" (1983)
This is one of the best electronic dance songs ever written. It features a constant rhythmic core, pounded out by a drum machine and mixed with various sequenced melodic sounds to create the feeling of a factory. Perfect synthesized dance music for the electronic '80s.

Pet Shop Boys, "West End Girls" (1985)
The Pet Shop Boys are Neil Tennant and Chris Lowe. What I really love about this song is how it "swings." Back in 1985, it showed that you could have a synth-pop song with an element of soul to it. Yes, it's electronic, but it also sounds smooth, moody, and funky.

Erasure, "Chains of Love" (1988)
Another synth-pop duo featuring Andy Bell (vocals) and one of the original members of Depeche Mode, Vince Clarke (keyboards). By the time this song was made in 1988, it was possible to make an entire pop dance song with many detailed parts all programmed within digital workstations.

LAB 50: THE SMITHS
THE SECOND BRITISH INVASION—POSTPUNK STYLE

Thanks to the rise of MTV Music Television, a number of British postpunk bands found a new level of success in the United States during the mid-1980s. These groups all presented a fresh feel for young audiences who had become tired of mainstream arena-style rock and roll.

The Cure, "A Forest" (1980)
This song was released as a single from the Cure's second album *Seventeen Seconds* and is a good example of the gothic rock sounds that were developing in England in the late 1970s. Listen to the sense of space and mood created in this song by the guitar and bass, and when lead singer Robert Smith begins to sing, his voice sounds distant and haunting.

The Psychedelic Furs, "Pretty in Pink" (1981)
This song actually inspired the 1986 film of the same name, and the film included a new recording of the song by the band. The song features an upbeat guitar-laden verse and a mellow, droning chorus.

Tears for Fears, "Everybody Wants to Rule the World" (1985)
This duo featuring Roland Orzabal and Curt Smith started as a postpunk synthesizer-based band but went on to be MTV superstars when this song hit the top of the charts in 1985. Despite the catchy nature of the song, the lyrics are quite deep, talking about the nature of power and how it can corrupt even the best of us.

Echo & the Bunnymen, "Lips Like Sugar" (1987)
This rock band formed in Liverpool in 1978, but the sound of their mid-'80s success has most defined them. This song features great, deep, meandering vocals from lead singer Ian McCulloch, and the sound of the clean, trebly guitars that were so common in postpunk rock.

LAB 51: R.E.M.
MUSIC INFLUENCED BY R.E.M.

R.E.M. inspired an entire generation of musicians who worked to combine the sounds of American roots music with an alternative rock sound.

Nirvana, "About a Girl" (1987)
Nirvana would become one of the biggest bands of the 1990s and radically alter the direction of rock and roll at the time. Kurt Cobain talked about this song being a perfect mix of his love for the Beatles and R.E.M. Listen closely. Can you hear how each of those artists are represented in this one song? If you can, listen to the excellent *MTV Unplugged* version of this song from 1994.

Pavement, "Unseen Power of the Picket Fence" (1993)
This song is actually about R.E.M. and Pavement's love for the album Reckoning. The song originally appeared on the compilation album called No Alternative, which featured various artists in support of AIDS relief.

The Decemberists, "Down by the Water" (2011)
The Decemberists use an Americana/folk rock sound that harkens back to some of the best of R.E.M., particularly the main melody sung by Colin Meloy. As it turns out Peter Buck is playing the twelve-string guitar on this track.

American Authors, "Best Day of My Life" (2013)
This alternative-indie-folk-rock band from Brooklyn, New York, performs in a style that owes a lot to R.E.M. The song starts with a catchy banjo part that serves as a main theme throughout the song. The lyrics lift you up and, when they are combined with the swinging rhythm part, it makes for the perfect feel good song.

LAB 52: U2
BANDS INFLUENCED BY U2

Here are a few of the many recent bands, who were influenced by the rock sounds of U2—and are proof that rock and roll is still going strong today.

Snow Patrol, "Chasing Cars" (2006)
This Irish band formed in 1994 and became a major player in the alternative rock scene in the early 2000s. The slow build to a powerful emotional and rocking end replicates the similar structures used by U2.

Coldplay, "Us Against the World" (2011)
This song comes from the 2011 concept album *Mylo Xyloto*. I like the directness of the music. The opening guitar sounds like the Edge, and the buildup in the second half could come right from the U2 album *The Joshua Tree*.

The Killers, "The Way It Was" (2012)
The Killers are the only American band on this list. On their early records, they had an uncanny ability to create songs that sounded new while creating a nostalgic aura for '80s music. This tune captures the sound of U2 in the rise and fall of the music and the grand scale of the "pull out all the stops" chorus.

Muse, "Madness" (2012)
Muse is an excellent British rock band. Many of their songs show the influence of U2, such as the song "Resistance" from 2009. "Madness" does not sound like most of Muse's other music, but it does show a particular influence from the Zooropa era of U2 and songs like "Numb" (1993).

⚡ ABOUT THE AUTHOR ⚡

Jason Hanley has loved music his entire life. As a child he attended concerts by Elvis Presley and Johnny Cash, and as a teenager he saw Yes and Depeche Mode. He completed his Ph.D. in musicology from Stony Brook University, where he wrote his dissertation entitled "Metal Machine Music: Technology, Noise, and Modernism in Industrial Music 1975–1996." He is currently the director of education at the Rock and Roll Hall of Fame and Museum in Cleveland, Ohio. In that position he teaches students of all ages in a wide range of educational programs and produces the museum's public programs. He has conducted oral histories and interviews with a variety of musicians, producers, and record industry professionals, including Les Paul, Little Anthony and the Imperials, Peter Hook, Darryl "DMC" McDaniels, DJ Spinderella, Alan Parsons, Dennis Edwards, Al Bell, Bill Kreutzmann, Tommy James, Spooner Oldham, and the band, Yes. He has taught courses in music history, electronic music, and popular music studies at Hofstra University, Stony Brook University, Cleveland State University, and Case Western Reserve University. Active in the music industry since 1988, he has played on, composed for, and produced numerous recordings and has performed live with many bands. When he is at home he loves to listen to music with his wife and four children—an activity that often includes singing and dancing, and an occasional quiz about music history.

⇥ ACKNOWLEDGMENTS ⇤

I would like to thank Janet Macoska for allowing me to use so many of her fantastic images (most of which were shot in Cleveland). Thank you to John Holstrum at *Punk* magazine and the Rock and Roll Hall of Fame.

Thank you to Joshua Rosenberg for his thoughtful comments during the copyediting, designer Leigh Ring for the beautiful layout, and Betsy Gammons for having patience during my writing process.

Thank you to my many music teachers over the years who helped me think about the sound of music, and how people use it, and to my friends and coworkers over the years with whom I've had many lively conversations and debates.

Thank you to my Mom and Dad, who helped to instill a love of music in me from a young age. And to my wife, Christine, and my children for being part of the process of writing the book—not to mention the birth of my son in the middle of the project!

Last, but certainly not least, I would like to thank my editor, Mary Ann Hall, who told me she wanted me to write a rock and roll book after we talked about music at a Fat Tuesday party. She helped develop the idea for this fantastic book which I have had so much fun writing.

PHOTOGRAPHER CREDITS

www.gettyimages.com:

Richard E. Aaron / Contributor, 74 (bottom)
Roberta Bayley / Contributor, 4–5; 68 (top); 74 (top)
Larry Burrows / Contributor, 48 (bottom)
Ed Caraeff / Contributor, 42 (top)
Charlie Gillett Collection / Contributor, 13; 16 (right); 56 (bottom)
John Coletti, 19 (bottom)
Consolidated News Pictures / Contributor, 62 (bottom)
David Corio / Contributor, 126 (top)
Fin Costello / Contributor, 102
Kevin Cummins / Contributor, 70 (top); 122 (bottom)
Donaldson Collection / Contributor, 23
Echoes / Staff, 87
Colin Escott / Contributor, 19 (top)
Evening Standard / Stringer, 24 (top)
Fotos International / Contributor, 116 (top)
GAB Archive / Contributor, 22 (bottom); 36 (bottom, left); 50 (top)
Gems / Contributor, 21; 62 (top)
Bobby Holland / Contributor, 94
Martha Holmes / Contributor, 17
Hulton Archive / Stringer, 32 (bottom)
Anwar Hussein / Contributor, 96 (top)
Dennis K. Johnson, 43
John P. Kelly / Contributor, 84 (bottom, right)
Keystone-France / Contributor, 3 (top, right)
KidStock, 8
David LEFRANC / Contributor, 12 (left)
Michael Ochs Archives, 3 (top, & bottom, left); 12 (right); 14; 15; 18; 20 (bottom); 28; 29; 30 (top & bottom, right); 32 (top); 36 (top & bottom, right); 40 (top); 48 (top); 49; 50 (bottom); 51; 55; 57; 58 (top); 60; 63; 64 (bottom, right); 82; 86 (top); 88 (bottom, left); 95; 100 (top & middle); 108 (top)
NBC / Contributor, 76 (top)

Terry O'Neill / Contributor, 26 (top)
Jan Persson / Contributor, 42 (bottom); 52–53; 64 (top)
Gilles Petard / Contributor, 20 (top); 22 (top); 44 (top); 54; 56 (top); 64 (bottom, left); 84 (bottom, left)
Popperfoto / Contributor, 24 (bottom); 96 (bottom)
Courtesy of *Punk* magazine, 68 (bottom)
Michael Putland / Contributor, 6 (bottom, right); 44 (bottom); 120 (top)
RB / Staff, 46; 112 (bottom)
Ebet Roberts / Contributor, 69; 72 (bottom); 124 (bottom)
Jack Robinson / Contributor, 86 (bottom)
Courtesy of the Rock and Roll Hall of Fame and Museum/ www.rockhall.com, 16 (left); 45; 128
Arthur Schatz / Contributor, 30 (bottom, left)
Frans Schellekens / Contributor, 76 (bottom)
Gus Stewart / Contributor, 84 (top)
Time & Life Pictures / Contributor, 6 (top); 90 (top)
Rob Verhorst / Contributor, 114 (top); 120 (bottom); 126 (bottom)
Chris Walter / Contributor, 38 (top); 47; 80 (top); 124 (top)
Julian Wasser / Contributor, 38 (bottom, left & right); 61
Stephen Wright / Contributor, 122 (top)

Janet Macoska Photography Inc./www.janetmacoska.com, 3 (bottom, right); 6 (bottom, left); 10–11; 26 (bottom); 27; 33; 34–35; 40 (bottom); 41; 58 (bottom); 66–67; 70 (bottom); 71; 72 (top); 78–79; 80 (bottom); 88 (top & bottom, right); 90 (bottom); 92–93; 98; 100 (bottom); 103; 104; 105; 106; 107; 108 (bottom); 109; 110–111; 112 (top); 114 (bottom, left & right); 116 (bottom); 118

~ INDEX ~

ONLINE PLAYLISTS

You can find the online playlists for this book at the following websites:

Spotify.com

Songza.com

You can listen to these playlists free of charge, or set up memberships on these services to have a more selective, ad-free experience.

You can also purchase individual songs or playlists from **iTunes**.

To hear the featured 52 songs from the book, search for the playlist:

We Rock! Book

All of the suggestions for additional listening songs in the Appendix are listed by chapter names.

We Rock! Book: Additional Listening, Rock & Roll Basics

We Rock! Book: Additional Listening, Rocking Out

We Rock! Book: Additional Listening, Deep Soul

We Rock! Book: Additional Listening, Punk Rock

We Rock! Book: Additional Listening, Dance Music

We Rock! Book: Additional Listening, New Rock Sounds

We Rock! Book: Additional Listening, New Wave